Strategic Learning Alignment

Make Training a Valuable Business Partner

Rita Mehegan Smith

Alexandria, Virginia

16 15 14 13 12 11 1 2 3 4 5 6 7 8

ASTD Press is an internationally renowned source of insightful and practical information on workplace learning and performance topics, including training basics, evaluation and return-on-investment, instructional systems development, e-learning, leadership, and career development.

Ordering information: Books published by ASTD Press can be purchased by visiting ASTD's website at store.astd.org or by calling 800.628.2783 or 703.683.8100.

Library of Congress Control Number: 2011922720

ISBN-10: 1-56286-740-7
ISBN-13: 978-1-56286-740-9

ASTD Press Editorial Staff:
Director: Anthony Allen
Manager, ASTD Press: Larry Fox
Project Manager, Content Acquisition: Justin Brusino
Senior Associate Editor: Tora Estep
Associate Editor: Ashley McDonald
Editorial Assistant: Stephanie Castellano
Copyeditor: Alfred Imhoff
Indexer: Abella Publishing Services, LLC
Proofreader: Abella Publishing Services, LLC
Interior Design and Production: PerfecType, Nashville, TN
Cover Design: Ana Ilieva Foreman

Printed by Versa Press, Inc., East Peoria, IL, www.versapress.com

To an extraordinary business leader, talent steward, and human being,
Herb L. Henkel, former CEO, Ingersoll Rand Company

Contents

Acknowledgments

This book exists because of special, talented people who have touched both my personal and professional life. First and foremost is Robert Preziosi, of Nova Southeastern University, my professional mentor and good friend. Eula Adams, my former boss and executive vice president of First Data Corporation, will always stand out as a brilliant leader who believed in learning and in the people he led. John J. Collins, my very first boss during high school, believed in my future and has encouraged me throughout my life.

Writing this book took perseverance, project planning, and the confidence to know it could be accomplished. For this, I thank Marcia Maytner, my fifth grade teacher. In her class, I completed a year-long research project that resulted in a 100-page report on the American Revolution. Her grade of A++ helped a little girl understand that she could literally write a book.

The many learning professionals with whom I worked over the years deserve a great deal of recognition and thanks. In particular, the members of the Ingersoll Rand University team have made world-class contributions to workplace learning and to the Ingersoll Rand business they serve. I am proud to work with this team.

The ASTD organization holds a special fondness in my heart. Through this organization, I have learned much about leadership, learning, and giving back to the learning profession. Thanks to Justin Brusino of ASTD Press, who provided enormous encouragement and wise counsel.

In addition, special thanks to my personal cheerleaders—my mom, Helen Mehegan, and my good friend, Monica Packenham. I wish that my father, John Mehegan, were alive to share in this experience. However, his love for me, his humor, and his value for learning are with me forever. Finally, last but not least, someone very special provides much joy in my life, my husband, Steve Proctor—I am grateful for your patience, encouragement, sense of humor, and love.

Introduction: Aligning Learning With Business—Move From Expense to Strategic Tool

Your senior executives are seated around the boardroom table conducting a business performance review. The economy is sluggish, and business results are not meeting previously forecasted numbers. The costs of the materials needed to manufacture your company's products have increased significantly from this time last year. A few months before the economic slowdown, your company acquired another large firm, resulting in billions of dollars in new debt. The chief financial officer and other senior executives are clearly concerned.

The senior executives at the table brainstorm various strategies to increase productivity to offset decreased sales and to pay down the debt. One leader suggests closing a handful of manufacturing sites. This would mean layoffs, but given that sales are down, this may be a necessary solution. Other ideas to reduce expenditures are examined. One of the newer senior executives asks, "Why don't we cut the training department? We could reduce or virtually eliminate it until the economy improves. Let's face it, training just isn't mission-critical to our business right now."

Silence hangs in the air. How would your organization's senior leaders respond to the recommendation to reduce or eliminate its learning function? Are you viewed as a cyclical expense or as a strategic tool vital to achieving the business goals?

Welcome to the "New Normal" for Learning

The recent recession triggered many such conversations in corporate boardrooms. In fact, according to Bersin & Associates' 2010 research report, "U.S. corporate training spending dropped 22 percent in the recession years of 2008 and 2009." Like the recession, this trend is similar worldwide. The "new normal" has upped the pressure to create business impact for the learning investment. The recession has created a new environment mandating that learning be laser focused on critical business issues, solve real business problems, and be delivered with increased speed and minimal interruption of work.

"Companies don't have enough time and resources to misapply efforts in learning; they are fighting for survival in an intensely competitive marketplace," Daniel Ramelli, vice president and chief learning officer of Fannie Mae, aptly stated in a 2008 essay. Simply put, businesses are requiring the learning function to become more tightly aligned with business goals than ever before.

Although the recent recession triggered this increased focus on alignment, in recent years business leaders have called more and more for increased linkages between learning and business results. For instance, virtually every CEO interviewed by Tony Bingham and Pat Galagan for ASTD's "At C Level Series"—originally published in *T+D* magazine and now available in a book (Bingham and Galagan 2007)—specifically articulates this need. Here are just a few examples:

- In 2007, McCormick's CEO, Robert Lawless, stated, "pick the best person you can find to lead your learning efforts. This person must have business acumen and the ability to link to strategies and the learning that's required to achieve them."
- In 2006, John Deere's CEO, Robert W. Lane, shared, "I want that individual to clearly understand the business objectives we are trying to accomplish."
- In 2005, Steelcase's CEO, James P. Hacket, added, "This connection between learning and strategy is becoming a CEO's mantra for how to direct a company."
- Finally, in 2004, Raytheon's CEO, Bill Swanson, stated, "I'm looking for my learning officer to be linked with the business president's. And by the way, our CLO and team are an expense to the company. They generate no profit on the work they do

inside Raytheon. They had better have a business case associated with their work."

The necessity for learning's increased alignment with business priorities is not a new conversation to learning professionals. A scan of conference brochures and presentation topics from the last decade reveals an increasing emphasis on aligning learning with business strategy. In a survey of learning executives by Brandon Hall (2005), "The Top Training Priorities for 2005," the results for 2004 and 2005 indicated that aligning learning with business goals consistently ranked as one of the top two priorities.

Why is alignment difficult to achieve? There are four main factors. First, many learning professionals simply do not view themselves as both businesspeople *and* learning experts. Many learning professionals speak in adult learning terms, not in the language of business. Second, those involved in the learning profession have not stepped up to operate at the same level of business rigor as their business partners. Learning professionals have not always been accountable for the kind of reporting needed for a solid business case with financial accountability. Third, many learning professionals provide training services rather than strategic learning. Strategic learning requires a learning function to form aligned partnerships at the most senior levels of a business. And fourth, many learning professionals perform activities to create alignment, but few use a powerful, systematic approach. These factors interact to create the alignment "abyss."

Stepping Up the Alignment Between Learning and Business Goals

In study after study, both business leaders and learning leaders consistently report that their number one challenge for the learning function is to strengthen its alignment with business goals. Given the increased demand for this alignment, it is of great concern that continued gaps in alignment are cited by both business leaders and learning leaders.

Many learning leaders use approaches that do create some alignment with business goals, such as governance councils or leaders serving as teachers. Yet these efforts are not creating full alignment. Although these are certainly good approaches, a more systematic process that will create deep and sustained alignment is required in today's business environment. But how can this process best be developed? The answer lies right before us. Borrowing from established business practices, those involved in the learning function can use the language, tactics, and tools of business as a system for creating powerful business alignment. This system is encompassed in the four-step Strategic Learning Alignment Model. What makes this SLA Model both unique and powerful is its business-oriented alignment practices and the integration of these practices into a highly logical, comprehensive system. Learning leaders finally have a detailed road map for creating alignment with their businesses' priorities.

How This Book Is Organized

This book is organized around the SLA Model, which provides a road map for your journey to unprecedented alignment with business strategies. A chapter is devoted to each of the model's four steps. In addition, the chapters offer a wealth of examples, tools, and interactive exercises. This book is designed for you to learn today and apply tomorrow.

To enable you to customize the information in the pages that follow to your specific needs, each chapter on the SLA Model can be used as a stand-alone piece. You may want to implement a group of key alignment strategies, or you may opt to employ the full power of the complete model.

Chapter 1 introduces the four steps of the SLA Model. You will gain understanding of how the four steps create a comprehensive system for achieving alignment between learning and business goals. In addition, you will come to understand why the model is designed to use the language, tactics, and tools of business. Using an approach already familiar to your business partners immediately increases your credibility with these business stakeholders. This chapter includes a self-assessment tool that will help you evaluate your current level of alignment with business strategy. This tool will serve as a customized learning guide for you as you move through the model.

Chapter 2, "Knowing Your Business," focuses on the information and knowledge you need to truly understand the issues and needs of your business partners. The chapter offers tools that will enable you to build a better understanding of how your business makes money. Thus, your company's business model, key business strategy, and metrics are distilled down to the critical few categories and further demystified for the non-financial layperson. Discussion questions and tools are provided to help you gain a deep understanding of your key stakeholders and to answer questions like "Who are they?" "What is important to them?" "How can you help them?"

Chapter 3, "Building the Business Case for Learning," offers three key ways to build your case: creating a strong value proposition statement, developing a business-focused annual learning plan for business leader prioritization, and drafting a strong business case to gain approval for a learning project. A value proposition framework is presented as a hands-on tool that will help you create your own succinct statement about your learning function's value to the business. The chapter also presents a high leader-engagement process for creating and prioritizing your annual learning plan. With assistance from a simple model and illustrated examples, you will be able to create a business-oriented annual learning plan that will increase your credibility and alignment with the business. The final method for building the case for learning is literally developing a case to fund a learning project. Using the language of business, you will learn how to create a strong case and increase the likelihood of its approval.

Chapter 4, "Engaging Leaders in Key Learning Activities," provides multiple methods for engaging leaders to create alignment. Engagement methods range from involving leaders in the governance of the learning function, to providing sponsorship, to joining rapid design teams, to inviting them to serve as visiting executives. Each method is described in detail, from its rationale for use through its full implementation. In addition, from a leader-as-teacher perspective, the chapter explains how to create a global Visiting Executive Program for powerful and intimate "fireside chats" between leaders and learning participants. The chapter closes with strategies to create a cachet for leaders engaged in your learning activities. Ways to integrate leadership engagement with other talent and recognition processes with your organization are discussed and illustrated. And the exercises provided will help you customize these engagement methods to your organization and current needs.

In chapter 5, "Communicating Your Business Results," you will learn multiple communication strategies to increase and sustain the "engagement mindshare" of your business leaders relative to learning. The chapter features a number of vivid case examples to illustrate an integrated and business-focused communication strategy for learning. Thus, you will learn how to develop the road map for your integrated communication system by creating an annual strategic communication plan for your learning. And you will discover how to segment your target communication audiences and to adapt your messages and media for maximum impact. The chapter also provides tips on crafting your message in the language of business and how to replicate the best practice of creating an annual report for your learning function. Moreover, you will find out how to create a "voice-of-the-customer" plan to continually capture and use the voice of your business partners as you manage your learning function. The chapter closes with pointers on creating an external relations communication plan for your learning group. These external acknowledgments further enhance your leaders' perception of your learning function as a valued partner.

Finally, chapter 6, "A Call to Action for Learning Leaders," offers a distillation of the book's findings and an invitation to consider your next steps in becoming the consummate rigorously strategic learning leader—including coaching notes for chief learning officers.

Chapter 1

The Strategic Learning Alignment Model

What's in this chapter:

- Why it's important to use the language and tools of business in making the case for the learning function and learning solutions.
- The components of the Strategic Learning Alignment Model.
- How to use the SLA Model.

■ ■ ■

Involving business leaders in learning is not a new idea. In fact, a variety of best practices can be used to align learning solutions with business priorities and leaders, including governance boards and leaders serving as teachers. Some learning professionals are at the beginning of their alignment journey. They may be using few or even no alignment practices. Others are using some practices and missing others. And still others are using many good practices in a series of events but have not leveraged these into an integrated operating system. Imagine the powerful alignment you could create by having an entire system of best practices as your road map. By capturing and organizing decades of best practices, this is exactly what the Strategic Learning Alignment (SLA) Model provides learning professionals.

Using the Language and Tools of Business

The SLA Model is unique in that it uses the language and tools that are already being used by your business leaders. The learning function is often viewed as lacking rigorous business discipline and processes. By using the language and tools of your business leaders, you build strong credibility. And rather than operating on parallel paths, learning and other business functions can form a highly integrated operating system.

Perhaps you entered the learning and development profession because you enjoyed the creativity of design, the interaction of the learning delivery, and the satisfaction of watching someone benefit from a learning program. Typically, our learning and development passion serves us well in our roles as specialists. However, we do operate within the world of business. Speaking the language of business is critical to our success. If you travel outside your home country, you know the benefit of communicating in the local language. I have personally experienced increased service, friendliness, and help from people when I attempt to communicate in their local language.

Like any specialists, it is easy for learning professionals to get caught up in the jargon of their profession. Have you ever overheard this type of conversation between a learning leader and a business leader?

Learning leader: We'll need to perform our full ADDIE process, to ensure that we are addressing the right learning competency. [ADDIE = analysis, design, development, implementation, and evaluation.]

Business leader: Hhmm. I just need them to increase their consultative selling skills so that we make our plan. What is the cycle time for this ADDIE thing? Is this something like our NPD—new product development cycle?

Learning leader: I believe they are similar. We can speed it up if we have full access to your key SMEs. Also, we can conduct a pilot first. This will give us some good formative evaluation data, and we can tweak the program from there.

Business leader: Hhmm. Aaaah. What is an SME?

Learning leader: Oh, sorry. An SME is a subject matter expert. They can help us understand the learning objectives. They can also advise us about the learning approaches that will be most effective for the salespeople, such as action learning, a blended learning solution, or on-the-job coaching.

Business leader: I will make sure you get your experts.

Learning leader: To make sure this program really makes the difference you are seeking, we will do a Level 3 and 4 evaluation about 90 days post program. Or do you think this should be longer, perhaps 180 days?

At this point, the business leader starts rubbing his or her forehead to alleviate the beginning pain of a learning-jargon headache!

Although this scenario is a bit exaggerated, I am sure some of it rang true for you. The learning leader definitely displayed his or her specialist expertise and made an effort to define the SME terminology. The business leader did attempt to understand the specialist terminology and even tried to relate the ADDIE process to his or her new product development business process. However, the failure to use the same language challenged the success of this conversation. The SLA Model will help you to become proficient in understanding what is important to your business leader and how best to communicate learning processes and outcomes in business terms.

Like most professions, business leaders use a set of tools and processes. Students enrolled in business schools are likewise taught how to use these. On a daily basis, business leaders use tools to assess data, make decisions, implement decisions, and measure success. Much rigor and process are required of business leaders by their stakeholders (management, customers, employees, shareholders, boards of directors).

Likewise, the learning and development profession has a set of tools and processes that we use with discipline and rigor. Although these are critical to creating successful learning solutions, they are unfamiliar to business leaders. In many cases, business leaders even view our tools and processes as nowhere near the level of rigor required of them from their stakeholders. How many times have you heard terms like "smile sheets" for our evaluation tools?

The *only* reason learning functions exist is to drive business outcomes. Therefore, it is our responsibility as learning professionals to become bilingual in both learning *and* business languages. In addition, to increase our level of communication and credibility with business leaders, it is our responsibility to use the tools and processes of business to augment our learning and development work. After all, learning *is* a *business process*.

Components of the Strategic Learning Alignment Model

The SLA Model is organized as a four-step process with various tactics and tools available for use at each step in the process. Figure 1-1 illustrates the model's four steps, starting with the oval at the top and moving clockwise.

Figure 1-1. The Strategic Learning Alignment Model

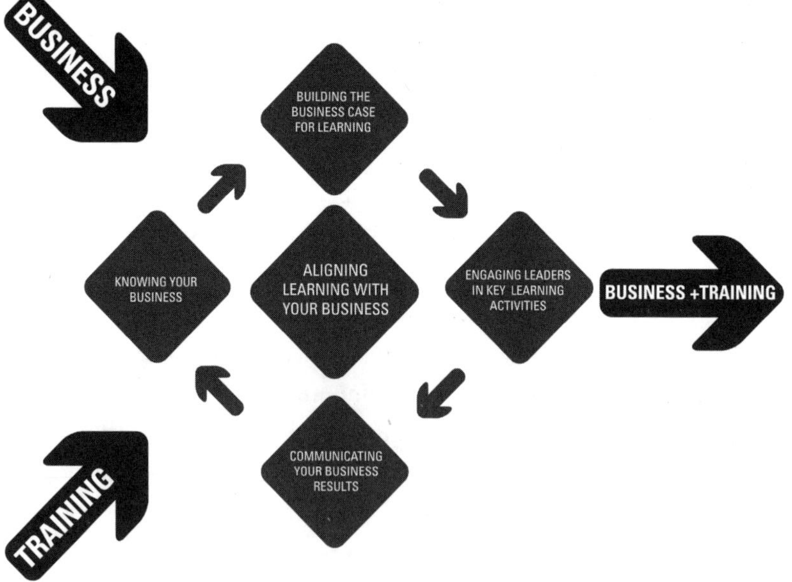

Step 1 of the SLA Model is *Knowing Your Business*, which provides a foundation for the other three steps. In business terms, this "knowing" is similar to "customer intimacy." Learning functions most definitely have customers and other key stakeholders. The business leaders are, in fact, your "customers." To be successful, businesses need to deeply understand customer needs and desired outcomes. This enables businesses to align products and services to meet these needs.

For example, Procter & Gamble has one of the world's largest and strongest portfolios of trusted retail brands. You are familiar with P&G if you have used any of its consumer products—Pampers, SafeGuard, Head & Shoulders, Pantene, or Oral B, to name just a few. A big part of P&G's ongoing success is its alignment with its customers' needs. It goes as far as having P&G employees live (or "embed" themselves) with various customer groups. This close contact allows these employees to directly observe and identify customers' needs. To align with business goals and deliver relevant, high impact learning solutions, learning professionals must have just as deep an understanding of their business.

Moving clockwise in figure 1-1, step 2 of the SLA Model is *Building the Business Case for Learning*. With a clear understanding of the issues facing business leaders, learning leaders are positioned to build their case for their learning solutions. Like other business leaders, learning leaders compete for funding from their company. In the P&G example, their depth of customer intimacy is used to create powerful and convincing business cases that P&G should invest in particular new products. Learning leaders also compete for business's "mindshare" and support for their learning initiatives among a pool of competing business priorities. This step in the SLA Model guides you in positioning your business value, capturing investment dollars, and communicating in the "local language" of your business.

With deep knowledge of your business and completion of a compelling business case, you are ready to move to step 3, *Engaging Leaders in Key Learning Activities*. This step helps you engage your leaders to create relevant learning solutions, gain sponsorship, and design and deliver learning solutions. The result of this engagement is strong alignment. Once again, P&G stands out as exemplary in the way they engage their customers. In fact, through a variety of processes and technologies, P&G partners with their customers to co-create and codevelop products. This fosters relevant, successful products that meet customer needs. In addition, with customers directly involved in the P&G design and development processes, increased customer loyalty results. In the pages that follow, you will learn about numerous methods, processes, and tools to help you create and maintain a similarly unprecedented level of engagement by your business leaders with your learning.

Step 4, the final step in the SLA Model, is *Communicating Your Business Results*. This important step helps you create a powerful brand for your learning, increase continued mindshare, and enhance your business leader's view of your learning function as a valued partner. For P&G, these activities are part of its marketing communication discipline, which involves a variety of tactics and tools, including tailoring messages for different segments of its customers, providing ongoing communication on the benefits and value of its products, using customer testimonials on the results produced, and linking its brands to various forms of external recognition and awards.

Using the SLA Model

The SLA Model offers a road map to achieving alignment between learning and business goals. The model contains a variety of processes and tools for your immediate use. As you familiarize yourself with these, you will be in a better position to assess your organization's readiness and resources to adopt these practices. Much like working your way along the buffet line at a restaurant, you may find yourself selecting a few key practices from each step of the model. Of course, second trips along the SLA Model "buffet line" are allowed and encouraged. In these subsequent trips, you may identify additional processes or tools appropriate for your current stage in the alignment journey.

Exercise for Understanding the Strategic Learning Alignment Model

Complete worksheet 1-1, a strategic learning alignment self-assessment. Use your score to identify areas of strength and opportunity in your current alignment with business.

Worksheet 1-1. Strategic Learning Alignment Self-Assessment
Select the response that most closely describes your learning function. Each question is worth up to two points. Upon completion, add up your score. For insight into your score, please see the "How Did You Score?" section at the end of this assessment.
1. How much of your learning content is related to real business issues? (2) Majority (1) Some (0) Very little
2. Which best describes your learning governance? (2) A mix of internal leaders and external thought leaders meeting with learning leaders on a regular annual basis (1) Internal leaders meeting with learning leaders on a regular annual basis (0) Internal leaders meeting with learning leaders ad hoc or seldom
3. How much of your learning is designed and delivered for minimal interruption to the workplace? (2) Majority (1) Some (0) Very little
4. When are you engaged by your business leaders to address learning needs? (2) When business strategy is formulated (1) When business strategy implementation is launched (0) When business strategy implementation is under way
5. What percentage of your learning solutions budget is allocated to strategic business needs? (2) Majority (1) Some (0) Very little

6. How often do you require learning requests to be accompanied by a business case? (2) Always (1) Sometimes (0) Seldom or never
7. Which best describes your approach to gather voice of customer (VOC) perception of the alignment of learning with business needs? (2) Regular, consistent process (1) Ad hoc (0) None in place
8. How knowledgeable is your learning staff in the key metrics of your business? (2) Strong (1) Average (0) Novice
9. What percentage of your or your learning leaders' time is spent working directly with business leaders? (2) Majority (1) Some (0) Little
10. How many of your business leaders are engaged in your key learning processes? (2) Majority (1) Some (0) Little
11. How would you describe your learning function's value proposition? (2) Explicit and understood by key business stakeholders (1) Explicit, but stakeholders' understanding could be improved (0) No value proposition currently in place
12. Which best describes how you communicate your value to business leaders? (2) Both operational reporting and strategic impact (1) Operational reporting only (0) Little or no value communication in place

13. To what extent are your leader engagement activities integrated into other talent management strategies (e.g., development opportunity for high potential leader)? (2) A great deal (1) Some (0) Few
14. On an annual basis, how much of your time do you spend implementing your learning function's alignment strategy and tactics? (2) Greater than 40 percent (1) More than 20 percent but less than 40 percent (0) Less than 20 percent
15. How would a majority of your executive leadership describe your learning function? (2) High value strategic tool (1) Adds some value (0) Low value cyclical expense
How Did You Score? Add up your scores from the self-assessment to see which category best describes your current state of alignment with business needs. Although piloted with many learning professionals, this self-assessment is non-scientific and is designed for directional feedback.
20–30: Succeeding Congratulations! You are using many strategies and tools to create alignment of your learning with business needs. However, there is still opportunity to further optimize your efforts into a complete, systematic approach. Which areas scored lowest? What can you do to increase these scores? How could you take your areas of success and better incorporate them into a complete, systems approach to alignment? This book will help you leverage your successes to achieve even stronger levels of alignment.

11–19: Improving
Good starting point! It's likely that you have some areas that are strong and others that could be improved. By addressing these areas for improvement, you will be moving toward a more complete, systematic approach to alignment. Are there lower scoring areas that could have a large impact on your alignment efforts? You will quickly find practical strategies and tools in this book to help you close these gaps.
0–10: Beginning
Good news? Yes, the good news is that by taking this self-assessment, you are aware of the importance of alignment and are already on your alignment journey. To accelerate your journey, look at the areas where you scored lowest. Are there immediate opportunities? This book is your alignment coach, guiding you each step of the way.

Chapter 2

Knowing Your Business

What's in this chapter:

- Understanding how your organization makes money and its business model.
- Understanding how your business tracks its money flow and ultimate net profit.
- How to identify and understand your stakeholders so you can increase their support and alignment with your businss goals.

■ ■ ■

The first step in the Strategic Learning Alignment Model is *Knowing Your Business*—the foundation on which you can build value for your business partners. Knowing your business is about understanding how your organization makes money, which includes understanding the key elements of revenue, expenses, and profit. It is also about understanding your business partners' key financial metrics and why these are important to them. This knowledge allows you to identify strategic opportunities for learning to add the most impact to your business. And it also enables you to speak the language of your key stakeholders and helps you build the business case for your learning solutions.

Mention business financials and the discomfort begins for many people as balance sheets, income statements, and financial ratios immediately come to mind. Rather than being an expert at calculating financial ratios or creating income statements, you need to interpret the basics of this financial data to spot issues and identify how business strategy, external trends, and the marketplace affect these numbers. No one, including your business partners, expects learning professionals to be financial experts. However, you do need to understand your organization's basic business model and business drivers. The good news is that only a *basic* understanding of business and financial data is required for learning professionals. To use an old adage, you don't need to know all the specifics of how your watch is made, you just need to know how to read the time.

For many years, business leaders viewed learning professionals solely as functional specialists or "trainers." As learning professionals, we have perpetuated this viewpoint by not readily identifying ourselves as businesspeople, not speaking the "language" of business, and not understanding or using the tools of business. However, where *do* we work? We work in *business*! We are both functional specialists and businesspeople. In the book *Finance Intelligence for HR Professionals* (Berman and Knight 2008, 21), John Hofmeister, the president of Shell Oil, sums this up aptly when he says that "anyone working in a business is a businessperson—so human resources people, for example, are businesspeople with a specialty in human resources."

A study by the U.S. Securities and Exchange Commission found that only half of all American adults could pass a basic financial literacy test. How many professionals sit in business meetings every day and don't understand a business concept or financial term? Not wanting to look stupid in front of others, they just keep quiet rather than ask for clarification. Learning professionals cannot afford to be in this silent group.

This chapter provides a basic primer on business acumen for the learning professional, in three sections:

- How does your business make money?
- What is your company's business model?
- How does your business track its money flow and ultimate net profit?

After we consider this business acumen primer, I've also included a section on strategies and tools for applying your business knowledge so that you can better understand your stakeholders' needs. In addition, we'll look at strategies and tools for managing your relationships with these stakeholders. You will find that the knowledge you gain from this chapter can be used in preparing business cases and communications for learning.

The statements in worksheet 2-1, a business language quiz, are direct quotations from business leaders captured from their conversations with learning professionals. These quotations are good examples of the language of business. Even if you score well on the quiz, this chapter will serve as a refresher. And if you miss any items in the quiz, by the close of this chapter you will have the knowledge to make the correct choices.

How Does Your Business Make Money?

Virtually every business involves revenue, expense, and profit. The money map, figure 2-1, uses the visual metaphor of a highway system to illustrate

Worksheet 2-1. Business Language Quiz
Match the numbered statements with the "translation" choices; each translation will only be used once. For the correct answers, see page 42—but don't peek before you try the exercise!
1. ____ "Our DSO ranks in the bottom third of our industry." 2. ____ "We're losing margin due to the increased prices of direct materials." 3. ____ "Revenue volume is up, but we're not seeing that transfer to price realization." 4. ____ "SG&A is increasing." 5. ____ "Channel development is key." 6. ____ "Inventory turns are slowing." 7. ____ "Our expense in warranties is trending upward from last year's figures."
Matching "translation" choices: A. Our profit is decreasing as we pay higher prices for manufacturing materials. B. We are not collecting our accounts receivables as fast as we should. C. We are incurring more costs due to poor quality of our products. D. Although our sales are high, our salespeople are offering too many discounts such as free freight. E. Profitable selling through our third party is important. F. Overhead costs are not trending positively. G. We are not syncing demand and timely delivery between our sales, warehouses, and operations.

how money flows through a business as revenue flows in, expenses flow out, and what remains is profit. This map of roads to profitability, which was created by the Business Literacy Institute, provides an easy-to-understand visual of how a business makes money.

Typically, a business is selling a product or service to a buyer for more than what it costs the business to make, sell, and deliver. The cash proceeds of the sale are referred to as revenue. However, this does not equal net profit (profit minus expenses) for the business. It costs money to make and sell the product or to deliver the service. Some of these costs are more directly linked to the making, selling, and/or delivery of the product or service. A few examples of these direct costs are materials, manufacturing labor, equipment, advertising, sales salaries, and commissions. There are also more indirect costs that go to support the overall business's efforts in making, selling, or delivering the product or service. Indirect costs are support or "administration," including such services as human resources, legal, training, and finance. The direct and indirect costs are subtracted from the revenue the seller received.

Business leaders view indirect or administrative costs as "overhead" and not directly related to generating profit. This underscores the importance of aligning your learning with the business to ensure that you are clearly contributing to achieving net profit. At the end of the day, this is what interests business leaders.

So, now that direct and indirect costs have been subtracted, does the business get its profit from the revenue it has collected? Not quite yet. There are still other expenses, such as interest on loans and taxes, that must be deducted. Then the business can collect its profit, which is referred to as its net profit. Viewed as a formula, this would be

$$\text{Profit} - (\text{Direct costs} + \text{Indirect costs}) = \text{Net profit}$$

These same basic building blocks of business exist whether the business is a company or a multinational Fortune 100 business. All these steps in the business process offer opportunities for you, as a learning professional, to affect the business's net profit. Understanding the basics of how your business makes its net profit is required for you to add value back to

Figure 2-1. The Money Map: The Roads to Profitability

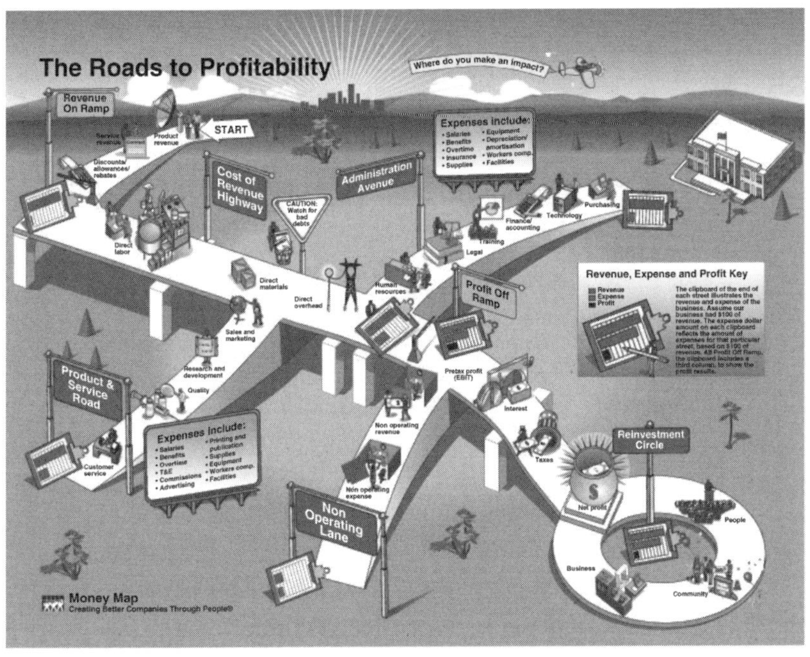

Source: Business Literacy Institute; used by permission.

the business. A host of other tools to build your business acumen can be found on the Business Literacy Institute's website (www.business-literacy .com). Different levels of stakeholders in your business will focus on different aspects of revenue, expenses, and profit. Senior leaders will focus on the entire "highway system" of profitability.

What Is Your Company's Business Model?

From the general components of any business (revenue, expenses, profit) we now move to the way a particular company makes money. This is called the company's business model. Think of a business model as a blueprint for how a company implements its strategy. It gives you a big-picture snapshot of your company's strategic priorities and how your company is designed to make money. Understanding how your company makes money is important for you as a learning professional. This knowledge can help you understand the key levers that drive the entire business, helping you to align your strategic learning solutions with these levers. In *Business Model Generation*, Alexander Osterwalder and Yves Pigneur (2009) identify nine building blocks of a business model:

- customer segments—customers grouped by common needs, behaviors, and attributes
- value propositions—how a product or service solves a customer's problem or satisfies a need
- channels—how a company communicates and reaches its customers
- customer relationships—the level of relationship, ranging from highly personalized to automated services
- revenue streams—cash generated from customer segments
- key resources—the physical, financial, and human resources required to implement the business model
- key activities—the most important actions for the company to operate successfully
- key partnerships—the company's network of suppliers and partners
- cost structure—the most important costs incurred for the company to operate successfully.

A familiar business model is that of Wal-Mart, the discount department store and chain of warehouses. In 2010, the Forbes Global 2000 (based on revenue size) named Wal-Mart the world's largest public corporation. Wal-Mart's business model is a low-price strategy, "everyday low prices." It accomplishes this through economies of scales in purchasing, advanced inventory and shelf management, and leveraging "float" or interest-free loans by paying its suppliers in 90 days while selling its products within seven days. Learning solutions for Wal-Mart will thus emphasize supply chain management to ensure that its purchasing and inventory capabilities are strong.

Gillette (owned by Procter & Gamble) uses a different business model. Gillette, which manufactures disposable razors and other personal care products, sells the razor handle at a low cost, knowing that its profit comes from sales of disposable blades that fit the razor handle. It spends a great deal of money on research and development and heavily patents its products to ensure that they dominate the razor blade market. Learning solutions for this type of business model will emphasize innovation and strategic product management.

The fast food giant McDonald's Corporation, the largest restaurant chain in the world, uses yet another type of business model. Its model is one of speed, quality, consistency, and real estate. Standardized meals and drinks produced with an assembly-line workflow create the speed—hence "fast" food. McDonald's uses standardization to create a consistent customer experience from one restaurant to another. It sets tight quality standards for its franchises. And its standardization of meals also allows it to gain economies of scale in food purchasing. A big part of its business

Figure 2-2. The Business Model Canvas

Key Partners (Company's network of suppliers and partners)	Key Activities (The most important actions for the company to operate successfully)	Value Propositions (How product or service solves a customer's problem or satisfies a need)	Customer Relationships (Level of relationship from highly personalized to automated services)	Customer Segments (Customers grouped by common needs, behaviors and attributes)
	Key Resources (Physical, financial, and human resources required to implement the business model)		Channels (How a company communicates and reaches its customers)	
Cost Structure (Most important costs incurred for the company to operate successfully)		Revenue Streams (Cash generated from customer segments)		

Source: "Business Model Canvas" (www.businessmodelgeneration.com). This work is licensed for public use under the Creative Commons Attribution-Share Alike 3.0 Unported License (http://creativecommons.org/licenses/by-sa/3.0/).

model is real estate, because it subleases to its franchisees. Knowledge of McDonald's business model helps those involved in the learning function understand the importance of and emphasize standard work practices.

In *Business Model Generation*, Osterwalder and Pigneur incorporate their nine business model building blocks into a visual Business Model Canvas, which is shown in figure 2-2. The business strategy and how the business is designed to make money are captured in a one-page snapshot.

Figure 2-3 depicts a Business Model Canvas for a personal products company. The company's business model emphasizes recurring revenue streams through disposable products. For the consumer, the initial razor handle purchase is inexpensive or even free. The ongoing, recurring purchase is the blades. The blades are disposable and are sold at a high margin or profit. Its key resources include a patent strategy that blocks other consumer product companies from gaining market share from this personal products company.

How Does Your Business Track Its Money Flow and Ultimate Net Profit?

Although the business model maps the *way* a business makes money, financial statements show you *how* the company is performing. Think of these financial statements as a scoreboard for business performance showing how money flows through a business, where it comes from, where it goes, and what ends up being net profit to the business. So to understand how your business tracks its money flow and ultimate net profit, you need to have a basic understanding of three main financial statements:

- the income statement
- the balance sheet
- the statement of cash flows.

Understanding the basics of these financial statements will help you answer these questions about your business:

- Is your business profitable?
- Are your revenues growing or decreasing?

Figure 2-3. A Business Model Canvas for a Personal Products Company

Key Partners (Company's network of suppliers and partners) *Manufacturers and retailers*	Key Activities (The most important actions for the company to operate successfully) *Marketing, research and development, and logistics*	Value Propositions (How product or service solves a customer's problem or satisfies a need) *Razor handle* *Blades*	Customer Relationships (Level of relationship from highly personalized to automated services) *Locked in with proprietary razor handle purchase*	Customer Segments (Customers grouped by common needs, behaviors and attributes) *Adult men primary segment, growing adult women segment in North America*
	Key Resources (Physical, financial, human resources required to implement the business model) *Brand and patents*		Channels (How a company communicates and reaches its customers) *Retail stores*	
Cost Structure (Most important costs incurred for the company to operate successfully) *Manufacturing, marketing, research and development, and logistics*			Revenue Streams (Cash generated from customer segments) ***One-time handle purchase, frequent blade replacements***	

Source: Adapted by the author from "Business Model Canvas" (www.businessmodelgeneration.com). This work is licensed for public use under the Creative Commons Attribution-Share Alike 3.0 Unported License (http://creativecommons.org/licenses/by-sa/3.0/).

- How effectively is your business using its assets?
- How efficient is your business in collecting the money it is owed by customers?
- How effective is your business in clearing out inventory?
- How effective is your business at controlling costs?

- Does your company have a low, moderate, or high rate of debt?
- How well is your business positioned to withstand an economic downturn?
- How does your business compare with other industry competitors?

It's not necessary that you memorize or practice calculating financial formulas; you just need to understand why a few of these data points are important to your business leaders. Don't sweat the formulas—just follow the money!

The examples used in the rest of this section represent financial statements from a multi-billion-dollar global industrial manufacturing company, "Company X." The company is fictional, but the financial statements are representative of a large manufacturing company. Many sources used to teach the basics of financial statements utilize overly simplified examples. Financial statements reflecting the simplicity of a teenager's lawn-mowing company do not remotely resemble the financial statements of more complex businesses. Though these do address the theory behind the financial statements, these simplistic examples do not prepare the learner to view and understand the real thing. In this book, we use real-life, publicly available financial statements, but do not identify the company.

Business is numbers oriented. Financial statements are used to report these numbers to assess business performance. To ensure alignment, learning professionals must understand the numerical performance metrics with which their business leaders are measured. By understanding the key financial indicators, a learning professional can track business trends and identify critical performance opportunities for the business. This enables the learning to support the business with strong alignment and a proactive approach to adding value.

The Income Statement: Is Your Business Profitable?

It is important for learning professionals to understand how profitable their company is at any given time. Imagine requesting a large learning investment from senior executives without knowing the state of the business. If profits are down, your investment request will only serve to highlight your disconnection from the business. *So instead, how can you, as a learning professional, proactively offer learning solutions to improve your company's levels of profitability?*

One tool for determining a company's profitability is its income statement. The income statement is sometimes referred to as a profit-and-loss statement, or P&L, or earnings statement. This statement shows revenues (sales), expenses, and profit for a defined period of time. Ultimately, it measures your company's profitability. Important components include the metrics of the *gross margin* and the *operating margin*. Figure 2-4 depicts an income statement.

Figure 2-4. A Sample Income Statement

Revenue money generated by the sales of products and services. Revenue is often called the "top line"

Operating income—the profit a company earns before it pays interest and taxes.

Discontinued operations—income/ expenses related to a portion of a company that has been sold or has stopped operating

Diluted EPS—a measure of earning per share that includes the dilutive effect if outstanding stock options or convertible deal

COMPANY X
CONDENSED CONSOLIDATED INCOME STATEMENT

In millions except per share amounts	Q3 2010	Q2 2010	Q1 2010
Net revenues	$ 3,730.3	$ 3,703.4	$ 2,953.4
Cost of good sold	(2,651.4)	(2,655.8)	(2,173.3)
Selling and administrative expenses	(670.7)	(664.6)	(646.6)
Operating income	408.2	383.0	133.5
Interest expenses	(70.2)	(71.1)	(712)
Other net	11.2	11.2	8.1
Earnings (loss) before income taxes	349.2	323.1	70.4
Provision for income taxes	(72.1)	(60.9)	(54.0)
Earning (loss) from continuing operations	277.1	262.2	16.4
Discontinued operations, net of tax	(39.5)	(60.3)	(10.4)
Net earnings (loss)	237.6	201.9	6.0
Less: Net earnings attributed to non controlling interests	(5.4)	(5.5)	(4.6)
Net earnings (loss) attributable to company X	$ 232.2	$ 196.4	$ 1.4
Amounts attributable to Company X ordinary shareholders:			
Continuing operations	$ 271.7	$ 256.7	$ 11.8
Discontinued operations	(39.5)	(60.3)	(10.4)
Net earnings (loss)	$ 232.2	$ 196.4	$ 1.4
Earnings (loss) per share attributable to Company X ordinary shareholders:			
Basic:			
Continuing operations	$ 0.84	$ 0.79	$ 0.04
Discuntinued operations	(0.12)	(0.18)	(0.04)
Net earnings (loss)	$ 0.72	$ 0.61	$ -
Diluted:			
Continuing operations	$ 0.80	$ 0.76	$ 0.04
Discontinued operations	(0.12)	(0.18)	(0.04)
Net earnings (loss)	$ 0.68	$ 0.58	$ -
Weighted average shares outstanding			
Basic	$ 324.7	$ 323.8	$ 322.7
Diluted	339.0	339.1	336.6
Dividend declared per ordinary shares	$ 0.07	$ 0.07	$ 0.07

Cost of goods sold (COGS)—costs directly associated with the fabrication of products or provision of services, Two examples are manufacturing labor and raw materials. They are referred to as "direct costs".

Net earnings (net income)—the "bottom line"

Source: Compiled by the author from publicly available generic data.

The Gross Margin

The gross margin measures your company's manufacturing and distribution efficiency during production. Higher margins show better performance. If your company has high gross margins, it will have more money left over to spend on other business operations, such as research and development or marketing.

Here are the basic aspects of the gross margin, organized as bare-bones formulas and sample calculations (note that Q1 = the first quarter of a four-quarter fiscal year, and that all revenues and cost of goods sold are in millions of dollars):

- Formula: (Revenue – Cost of goods sold) / Revenue.
- Purpose: Measures the percentage of sales retained after production costs are incurred.
- Q1 2010: (2,953.4 – 2,173.3) / 2,953.4 = 26.4%.
- Q2 2010: (3,703.4 – 2,655.8) / 3,703.4 = 28.3%.
- Q3 2010: (3,730.3 – 2,651.4) / 3,730.3 = 28.9%.
- Q2 2010 average among Company X's peer companies: 31.2%.

The Operating Margin

Operating margins measure your company's pricing strategy and operating efficiency. Again, higher margins are better. Your business leaders look closely at the operating margin to determine if their pricing management is effective. They also look at the operating margin to determine if the operating expenses of the company are too high. These expenses include selling, general, and administrative costs, referred to as SG&A. The learning function is typically considered part of SG&A, or "overhead."

Here are the basic aspects of the operating margin, again organized as bare-bones formulas and sample calculations (note that Q1 = the first quarter of a four-quarter fiscal year, and that all revenues and cost of goods sold are in millions of dollars):

- Formula: Operating income / Revenue.
- Purpose: Measures the profitability of a company before interest and tax expenses.
- Q1 2010: 133.5 / 2,953.4 = 4.5%.
- Q2 2010: 383.0 / 3,703.4 = 10.3%.
- Q3 2010: 408.2 / 3,730.3 = 10.9%.
- Q2 2010 average among Company X's peer companies: 11.8 percent.

Earnings per Share From Continuing Operations

Most income statements include a calculation of earnings per share, or EPS. This calculation tells you how much money shareholders would receive for each share of stock they own if the company distributed all its net income for the period.

Here are the basic aspects of earnings per share, again organized as bare-bones formulas and sample calculations (note that Q1 = the first quarter of a four-quarter fiscal year, and that all revenues and cost of goods sold are in millions of dollars):

- Formula: Net earnings attributable to company shareholders / Weighted-average diluted shares outstanding.
- Purpose: Measures the profitability of a company.
- Q1 2010: 11.8 / 336.6 = $0.04.
- Q2 2010: 256.7 / 339.1 = $0.76.
- Q3 2010: 271.7 / 339 = $0.80.

Summing Up

Why are an income statement and its key metrics useful to a learning professional? Understanding the components of profitability enables a learning professional to identify learning solutions that will drive increased profit. For example, if operating margins are lower than forecast, a number of potential learning solutions could be applicable. Perhaps the sales force is discounting products at a high rate, causing decrease margins. Possible learning solutions on negotiation skills and pricing management could be useful here. If the G&A (general and administrative costs) are higher than target, there is an opportunity to reduce the expenses incurred by your learning function. Perhaps you could increase your use of virtual delivery to decrease overall company travel expenses. Or minimally, you may delay your request for additional headcount resources for your learning function.

The Balance Sheet: What Is Your Company Worth?

As a learning professional, you need to understand what your company owns and what it owes at a given point in time. In addition to understanding what is needed to drive profitable growth, learning professionals should also be aware of how much debt and other liabilities it takes to create that profit. If their company has a heavy amount of debt, it would not be wise for a learning leader to request a large dollar investment that would require the company to borrow even more funds. Through understanding a company's debt and other liabilities, a learning professional can provide learning solutions resulting in improved time to payment from customers or in increased movement of inventory into cash. The company balance sheet provides this information for the learning professional.

The company balance sheet, shown in figure 2-5, depicts your company's financial position, including what it owns, what it owes, and the amount invested by shareholders. In other words, it tells what your company is worth. There are three major parts to the balance sheet: assets, liabilities, and shareholder's equity. By design, the balance sheet must balance. The balance sheet goes beyond the income statement, which shows only profit. The balance sheet shows your company's amount of debt. Your company could be making a profit, but it could also have high debt to fund the business operations.

The Debt-to-Equity Ratio

Your company's assets (items of economic value) should be greater than its liabilities (debt). This allows your company to withstand periods of

Figure 2-5. A Sample Company Balance Sheet

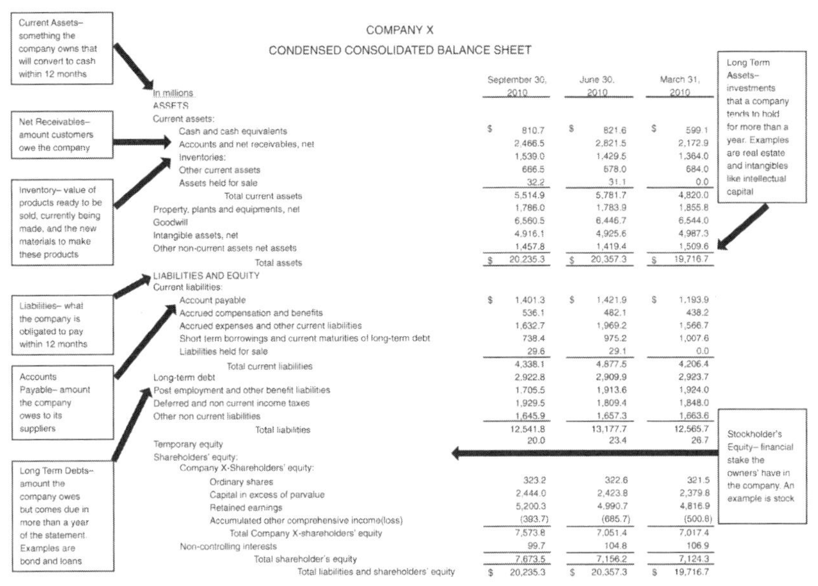
COMPANY X

CONDENSED CONSOLIDATED BALANCE SHEET

In millions	September 30, 2010	June 30, 2010	March 31, 2010
ASSETS			
Current assets:			
Cash and cash equivalents	$ 810.7	$ 821.6	$ 599.1
Accounts and net receivables, net	2,466.5	2,821.5	2,172.9
Inventories:	1,539.0	1,429.5	1,364.0
Other current assets	666.5	678.0	684.0
Assets held for sale	32.2	31.1	0.0
Total current assets	5,514.9	5,781.7	4,820.0
Property, plants and equipments, net	1,786.0	1,783.9	1,855.8
Goodwill	6,560.5	6,446.7	6,544.0
Intangible assets, net	4,916.1	4,925.6	4,987.3
Other non-current assets net assets	1,457.8	1,419.4	1,509.6
Total assets	$ 20,235.3	$ 20,357.3	$ 19,716.7
LIABILITIES AND EQUITY			
Current liabilities:			
Account payable	$ 1,401.3	$ 1,421.9	$ 1,193.9
Accrued compensation and benefits	536.1	482.1	438.2
Accrued expenses and other current liabilities	1,632.7	1,969.2	1,566.7
Short term borrowings and current maturities of long-term debt	738.4	975.2	1,007.6
Liabilities held for sale	29.6	29.1	0.0
Total current liabilities	4,338.1	4,877.5	4,206.4
Long-term debt	2,922.8	2,909.9	2,923.7
Post employment and other benefit liabilities	1,705.5	1,913.6	1,924.0
Deferred and non current income taxes	1,929.5	1,809.4	1,848.0
Other non current liabilities	1,645.9	1,657.3	1,663.6
Total liabilities	12,541.8	13,177.7	12,565.7
Temporary equity	20.0	23.4	26.7
Shareholders' equity:			
Company X-Shareholders' equity:			
Ordinary shares	323.2	322.6	321.5
Capital in excess of parvalue	2,444.0	2,423.8	2,379.8
Retained earnings	5,200.3	4,990.7	4,816.9
Accumulated other comprehensive income(loss)	(393.7)	(685.7)	(500.8)
Total Company X-shareholders' equity	7,573.8	7,051.4	7,017.4
Non-controlling interests	99.7	104.8	106.9
Total shareholder's equity	7,673.5	7,156.2	7,124.3
Total liabilities and shareholders' equity	$ 20,235.3	$ 20,357.3	$ 19,716.7

Source: Compiled by the author from publicly available generic data.

financial problems, such as a recession. When your company seeks loans, the prospective lenders look to see if your company's balance sheet has manageable levels of debt compared with its assets. This signals your company's ability to repay its debt.

Here are the basic aspects of the debt-to-equity ratio, again organized in a simple formula and sample calculations (note that Q1 = the first quarter of a four-quarter fiscal year, and that all revenues and cost of goods sold are in millions of dollars):

- Formula: Total liabilities / Shareholders' equity.
- Purpose: Measures the amount of debt and equity financing a company is using.
- Q1 2010: 12,565.7 / 7,124.3 = 1.8.
- Q2 2010: 13,177.7 / 7,156.2 = 1.8.
- Q3 2010: 12,541.8 / 7,673.5 = 1.6.

Days Sales Outstanding

Anything your company owns that can potentially generate cash is considered an asset. Assets are listed on the balance sheet in order of how easily they can be converted to cash. Assets include the money owed your company by customers who purchased products or services on credit, known as accounts receivable. If customers do not pay on time, your company cannot pay other debts, because it has money tied up in the customers' products or services. You want to see a high turnover, or shorter time elapsing between the customers' receipt of products or services and payment of the invoice or bill. The more quickly your company can collect its accounts receivable, the less money it has tied up in these receivables and the more money it can use to pay its debts or reinvest in the company.

Here are the basic aspects of days sales outstanding, presented in a simple formula and with sample calculations (note that Q1 = the first quarter of a four-quarter fiscal year, and that all revenues and cost of goods sold are in millions of dollars):

- Formula: (Period ending net receivables balance / Current quarter revenues annualized) * 365.
- Purpose: Measures the average number of days a company takes to collect cash after a sale has been made.
- Q1 2010: (2,172.9 / 2,953.4 * 4) * 365 = 67 days.
- Q2 2010: (2,821.5 / 3,703.4 * 4) * 365 = 69 days.
- Q3 2010: (2,466.5 / 3,730.3 * 4) * 365 = 60 days.
- Q2 2010 average among peer companies: 59 days.

Inventory Turns

Another measurement of good asset management is how quickly your company sells its inventory of products. The faster your company turns over (sells) inventory (sells), the less money your company has tied up in its inventory. The longer inventory sits on your shelves, the longer the money invested in this inventory is unavailable to your company.

Here are the basic aspects of inventory turns, organized as a barebones formula with sample calculations (note that Q1 = the first quarter of a four-quarter fiscal year, and that all revenues and cost of goods sold are in millions of dollars):

- Formula: Current quarter cost of goods sold annualized / Period ending inventory balance.
- Purpose: Measures the number of times inventory is used in a period of time.
- Q1 2010: (2,173.3 * 4) / 1,364.0 = 6.4 turns.
- Q2 2010: (2,655.8 * 4) / 1,429.5 = 7.4 turns.
- Q3 2010: (2,651.4 * 4) / 1,539.0 = 6.9 turns.
- Q2 2010 average among peer companies: 6.8 turns.

Summing Up

Why are a balance sheet statement and its key metrics useful to a learning professional? Understanding how your company's assets (items of economic value) compare with its liabilities (debt) helps you target learning that increases assets and decreases reliance on debt. For example, you might provide learning to the employees in the Accounts Receivable Department on how to negotiate payment from a customer. In another example, you could provide learning on integrated planning targeted to managers in sales, inventory, and operations. This could be an optimal time to demonstrate your learning function's effectiveness at streamlining key processes, resulting in financial savings for the company.

The Cash Flow Statement: How Does Your Company Source and Use Cash?

Understanding how cash flows in and out of the company helps the learning professional understand the health of a business and the strategic priorities of the business leaders. Is the company generating cash from its operations, signaling an efficiently run workplace? To what extent is the company investing its cash in research and development, signaling growth? Does the company have a high level of debt to pay down, signaling high interest expenses and limiting other investments? The cash flow statement provides answers to these questions.

The cash flow statement shown in figure 2-6 reports the cash generated and used during the time interval specified in its heading. The cash flow statement shows how a company is paying for its operations and future growth by detailing the "flow" of cash between the company and the outside world. Positive numbers represent cash flowing in; negative numbers represent cash flowing out. Simply put, this statement tells you where money comes from and where it is spent by organizing and reporting the cash generated and used in these three categories:

- *Operating cash flow*—often referred to as working capital—is the cash flow generated from internal operations. It includes the cash used to run the business; cash coming in from sales of the product or service; and cash going out to pay for salaries, vendors, raw materials, and the like.
- *Investing cash flow* is generated internally from nonoperating activities. It includes capital investments in plant and equipment or other fixed assets, or investment in research and development.
- *Financing cash flow* is the cash going to and coming from external sources, such as lenders, investors, and shareholders.

The most important of these three categories is cash flow from operating activities. A company needs to generate cash from its operations and cannot sustain itself on borrowing or its financial investments. You want the cash flow from operations to be at least equal to the net income profit. This tells you that the company is generating at least as much cash as it is reporting in its net income (profit) earnings. A company with a more positive cash flow is effective at turning its profits into cash. Having more cash available internally reduces the need for a company to borrow money and pay high interest rates.

The Return on Invested Capital

The return on invested capital (ROIC) is a commonly used financial measure that quantifies how well a company generates cash flow relative to the capital it has invested in its business. ROIC, in basic terms, is the

Figure 2-6. A Sample Cash Flow Statement

Net earnings from the income statement

Cash from Operating Activities–Examples are customer payments into the company and salaries and cost for vendors out of the company

Cash from Investing Activities–Examples are the company's investment in capital assets like a truck or equipment.

Cash From Financing Activities–Examples are the company's borrowing and paying back loans. Also it is the sale of stock and dividends paid out.

COMPANY X
CONDENSED CONSOLIDATED STATEMENT OF CASH FLOWS

In millions	Three months ended		
Cash flows from operating activities:	September 30, 2010	June 30, 2010	March 31, 2010
Net earnings (loss)	$ 2376	$ 2020	$ 60
(Income) loss from discontinued operations, net of tax	4260	6470	1040
Adjustments loan and cash provided by (used in) operating activities:			
Depreciation and accomodation	1070	1103	1121
Stock scaled share-based compensation	120	151	194
Changes in other assets and liabilities, net	(176.3)	(182)	(2426)
Other, net	647	(26.6)	423
Net cash provided by (used in) continuing operating activities	2876	3,473	(524)
Net cash provided by (used in) discontinued operating activities	(295)	(261)	(100)
Cash flows from investing activities:			
Capital expenditures	(450)	(380)	(34.3)
Proceeds from sales of property, plant and equipment	6.9	86	(33)
Acquisitions, net of cash acquired	-	(72)	17
Other, net	-	-	-
Net cash provided by (used in) continuing increasing activities	(381)	(36.6)	(35.9)
Net cash provided by (used in) discontinued increasing activities	07	(0.3)	-
Cash flows from financing activities:			
Proceeds from issuance of bonds	-	-	-
Proceeds from bridge loan	-	-	-
Payments of bridge loan	-	-	-
Commercial paper program (net)	-	(69.5)	695
Other short-term borrowings (net)	98	100	41
Proceeds from long bridge loan	128	198	190
Payments of long-term debt	(2516)	(94)	(2621)
Net change in debt	(2290)	(491)	(1695)
Statement of cross currency swap	-	-	-
Debt issuance costs	-	(55)	-
Dividends paid in ordinary shareholders	(227)	(225)	(225)
Dividends paid on non-controlling interest	(10)	(8.4)	-
Acquisition of non-controlling interest	(80)	(10.4)	104
Proceeds from camrose of stock options	104	387	(16)
Net cash provided by (used in) continuing financing activities	(2503)	(37.2)	(1832)
Net cash provided by (used in) discontinued financial activities	-	-	-
Effect of exchange rac changes on cash and cash equivalent	187	(46)	39
Net increase(decreased) in cash and cash equivalents	(109)	2225	(2776)
Cash and cash equivalents-beginning of period	8216	9991	8762
Cash and cash equivalents-end of period	$ 8107	$ 8216	$ 9991

Source: Compiled by the author from publicly available generic data.

amount of profit that a company earns for every $1.00 of capital invested in the business.

Here is the formula to calculate ROIC, accompanied by sample calculations (note that Q1, Q2, and Q3 indicate the particular quarter of the four-quarter fiscal year, and that the figures in the formula are in millions of dollars):

- Formula: Trailing quarter operating income (after tax) annualized / Period ending invested capital.
- Invested capital = Net receivables + Net inventory + Prepaid expenses and other current assets + Total noncurrent assets

– Accounts payable – Accrued compensation and benefits – Other accrued expenses.

- Purpose: Measures the return management is generating on company-funded investments.
- Q1 2010: (133.5 * 0.80)*4) / (2,172.9 + 1,364.0 + 684.0 + 14,896.7 – 1,193.9 – 438.2 – 1,566.7) = 2.7%.
- Q2 2010: (383.0 * 0.80)* 4) / (2,821.5 + 1,429.5 + 678.0 + 14,575.6 – 1,421.9 – 482.1 – 1,969.2) = 7.8%.
- Q3 2010: (408.2 * 0.80)* 4) / (2,466.5 + 1,539.0 + 666.5 + 14,720.4 – 1,401.3 – 536.1 – 1,632.7) = 8.2%.
- Q2 2010 average among peer companies: 8%.

Summing Up

Why are a cash flow statement and its key metrics useful to a learning professional? Determining whether your company has a healthy cash flow can help you target high value learning solutions to increase positive cash flow. For example, you could provide learning for the entire workforce on how each employee contributes to positive cash flow. Each employee could enter a specific action and potential range of savings. Partnering with the Finance Department, you could track these quantitative improvements to cash flow. Recognizing cash flow opportunities and proactively recommending suitable learning solutions will strengthen your alignment with business partners.

Identifying and Understanding Your Stakeholders

The business acumen primer you have just reviewed will help you better understand the needs and wants of your key stakeholders, which is critical to your creating alignment with these stakeholders. Imagine living in a foreign country and not understanding the local language. How well would you truly get to know the local people? It is the same premise for learning professionals with our key stakeholders.

There are various definitions of stakeholders. Stakeholders typically have an interest (or stake) in a project, process, or initiative. They can be both internal and external to the organization. Here is a quick checklist to help you identify if a person or group is your key stakeholder:

- Do they control the resources you need or use?
- Can they block your project (process, initiative), either directly or indirectly?
- Do they have approval power over your work?
- Do they own a key process affected by your work?
- Do they have influence that shapes the thinking of other key stakeholders?

If you answered yes to any of these questions, you identified a stakeholder in your learning function. The learning function has a number of key stakeholders—including the CEO, other senior leaders, human resource leaders, information technology leaders, finance leaders, purchasing/sourcing leaders, employee managers, end users of the learning solutions, and external vendors, just to name a few. Within these groups are people who are more influential than other stakeholders. The sidebar on pages 38–39 gives a true scenario of a time, early in my career, when I did not understand the value of stakeholder management.

Once you identify and assess your key stakeholders, you are in a stronger position to align with and address their interests and concerns. In addition, you can now customize their engagement in your learning processes to match their interests and concerns. It is useful to ask others to provide input into your stakeholder identification and assessment. With this additional help, you may gain valuable new perspectives about the stakeholders. These aspects are explored further in worksheet 2-2 on stakeholder analysis.

Managing Stakeholders

The company was a large financial services organization that had just made a large acquisition. I was hired by its largest division—reporting to the division's president—to help transform it into a customer-focused organization. The president was passionate about driving excellence, including our many customer service call centers, and he provided the funds to invest in top-notch learning solutions. I was co-located with him in the corporate office—sounds ideal.

I did not fully sense that he was a new leader to the company and thus had not fully built alignment with his vision among the other division leaders. But I began driving the customer-focused transformation, and it did not take long for me to hit a speed bump.

The division's existing leadership team was a legacy from the acquired company. Although the team's members nodded agreement with the new division president, their actions were the opposite. For instance, a train-the-trainer model was a key part of the learning rollout. The division's call center leader—who was influential and outspoken—would rescind her resources at the last minute due to ostensible call volume increases and pull certified trainers into different, nontraining roles. This left me with canceled classes, wasted expenses, and little progress at the call center. Another key influencer was the head of finance. He felt all learning solutions were a complete waste of time and conveyed this openly and often. He made requesting funds for the transformation a complete nightmare. But the division president did not see this blocking behavior of his finance person and call center leader. I was convinced the answer was for me to quit the company.

At the time, I was in graduate school and was taking a course on organizational development, much of which was dedicated to managing change. The change management concepts started to sink in, I was exposed to stakeholder mapping as a tool to create alignment for change, and I began to use it at my current company. I could instantly see the landscape of stakeholders, their influence, and their level of support for customer-centered learning.

The call center leader was neutral at best toward the customer-focused transformation. But why was this happening? With further thought, I realized that she felt that the new division president and his new team were actually critiquing her leadership of the call center. She believed that she already had working solutions to drive customer excellence, and that this transformation had been imposed on her. Furthermore, I discovered that she had repeatedly asked for a capital expenditure to upgrade her facility but that it had been denied due to the company's overall finances. How could I move her from a neutral level of nonopposition (I was optimistic) to a favorable level?

First, I formed a governance group, ensured that she had a key role, and asked the division president to sponsor it. We worked together to identify the why and the how of the customer-focused transformation. I shared with her the positive financial impact this initiative could have on reducing customer-mishandling calls and related fines. If she could be perceived as driving increased operating and financial performance, she might get the funds for her capital expenditure vision. Over time, she clearly began to feel part of the solution. I made sure that the division president recognized her efforts and was careful to manage the transformation as building on her past good work while moving us to an even greater customer focus. I positioned the train-the-trainer role as a high potential opportunity and retention tool, so the training skills could transfer beyond the current customer-focused initiative and help her build her own stronger training team.

Now, how could I reach the finance leader? He viewed the learning solutions and me as overhead expense. He was concerned that the fines we paid for poor customer service were negatively affecting our operating income. Certainly costly fines were negatively affecting the profit we generated from running the company. Armed with this knowledge, I pulled together the business reasons why we needed this transformation. Working with my division president, I presented this data at a monthly financial review meeting. We could clearly reduce the customer call mishandling errors that resulted in fines for us from the banks we served. This attracted his attention. In effect, even a 10 percent reduction in call mishandling fines would easily pay for the entire learning solution. I asked the finance leader to join our steering committee and sponsor our learning effectiveness measurement activities. He helped set the metrics and personally monitored the result.

By identifying who wielded the greatest influence, assessing their current level of support, and understanding their stake in the learning solutions, I was able to persuade the call center leader and the division's other blockers to become supporters. A key factor is applying your understanding of how your business makes money and what performance metrics are most important to each stakeholder. The call center leader connected with the increased cash flow available from reduced fines and how this could be repositioned for a capital expense. The finance leader was focused on increasing earnings and reducing costs such as fines. Stakeholder management became a standard activity of the customer-focused transformation project and my learning function. We did achieve the results we targeted. I had the support and engagement of these two leaders throughout my tenure with this company. It was well worth the time it took to identify, assess, and manage my key stakeholders.

Worksheet 2-2. Stakeholder Analysis

Use this stakeholder analysis tool to assess your stakeholders and their level of influence. Engage other team members and leaders to help you with this exercise. Also, note the 1–5 rating on level of influence. The red, yellow, and green status rating shows current level of support of each stakeholder. Red indicates the stakeholder views your activity in a negative way; yellow indicates he or she is neutral, and green means the training is viewed favorably. The goal is to move all stakeholders to green.

Stakeholder Analysis: Use the worksheet to list stakeholders and assess their influence and supportiveness of the change initiative.

Stake-holder	Role	Influence (1-5)	Unfavorable	Neutral	Favorable	Follow-Up Actions	Who	Date	Status
Stake-holder name	Role in the organi-zation	Rate this individual's level of influ-ence in the organization: 1 = no/little Influence; 5=highly influential	Place an "X" in the box that most closely depicts this individual's attitude toward the change initiative.			Consult the matrix for tips on how to influence different stakehold-ers.	Team member account-able	Due date	Status (red, yellow, green)
									Red
									Yellow
									Green

A person or group that fits one or more of these criteria should be on your stakeholder list:

- Controls critical resources
- Can block the change directly or indirectly
- Must approve certain aspects of the change
- Shapes the thinking of other critical constituents
- Owns a key process that is affected by the change.

Keep this document confidential!

Engaging business leaders in your key learning activities—such as governance, program design, and/or leaders as teachers—are all strategies to manage your stakeholders (see chapter 4). In the customer-focused transformation scenario highlighted earlier in the sidebar, the call center leader was recruited to serve on a learning governance board to increase her exposure to champions and to engage her in steering the learning solutions associated with the customer-focused transformation initiative.

Key Points for Knowing Your Business

- Business acumen is critical to creating alignment of learning with the business. Learning professionals are *both* functional specialists and businesspeople.
- Learning professionals need to know the basics of how any business makes money. Three important components are revenue, expense, and profit.
- In addition, learning professionals need to understand the business strategies and how their business implements this strategy. This is referred to as the company's business model. A business model describes the way a particular company makes money.
- Financial statements are scoreboards for business performance, showing how the company is performing. The three key financial statements are the income statement, the balance sheet, and the cash flow statement. These will tell you if your company is profitable, what it is worth, and how it sources and uses cash.
- To truly know your business, you must know what aspects of the business are important to your various stakeholders. These are people who have a vested interest in your project, process, or initiative.

Exercise 1: How Does a Business Make Money?

Using the money map in figure 2-1 above, identify how your learning function can add value to the key elements of revenue, expense, and profit depicted on the map.

Exercise 2: Understanding Your Company's Business Model

Using the business model canvas in figure 2-2 on page 23, below complete the nine building blocks for your business. To gain feedback on your responses, review your completed Business Model Canvas with a business partner. An additional option is to repeat this exercise with your learning team.

Note: A poster-size copy of this business model canvas is available at www.businessmodel generation.com. For the conditions of use, see http://creativecommons.org/licenses /by-sa/3.0/ke 3.0Unported License.

Exercise 3: Using Financial Statements for Further Analysis

Using the sample financial statements and referring to the accompanying text in this chapter, answer the following questions about this sample business. These questions should look familiar because they are the same questions that opened the discussion of financial statements in this chapter. (The correct answers are included at the end of these exercises.)

- Is the company profitable?
- Are its revenues growing or decreasing?
- How efficient is the company in collecting the money it is owed by customers?
- How efficient is the company in clearing out its inventory?
- How effective is the company at controlling costs?
- Does the company have a low, moderate, or high rate of debt?
- How well is the company positioned to withstand an economic downturn?
- How does the company compare with other industry competitors?

Exercise 4: Identifying and Understanding Your Stakeholders

Use the stakeholder analysis in worksheet 2-2 to identify and analyze two or three of your key stakeholders.

The correct answers to exercise 3 above on using financial statements for further analysis:

- Is the company profitable? YES. See the operating margin on the income statement.
- Are the revenues growing or decreasing? GROWING. Slight growth over previous quarter. See the net revenues on the income statement.
- How efficient is the company in collecting money it is owed from customers? SLIGHTLY BELOW AVERAGE. The company's best performance was 60 days, while the peer average is 59 days. Calculated from the balance sheet—days sales outstanding.

- How efficient is the company in clearing out its inventory? ABOUT AVERAGE WITH ITS PEER COMPANIES. The company's last inventory turn performance was 6.9 turns. Peer companies average 6.8 turns.
- How effective is the company at controlling costs? BELOW ITS PEER AVERAGE. Peer companies average 11.8% operating margin, while the company's last quarter performance was 10.9%. This is calculated from the income statement.
- Does the company have a low, moderate, or high rate of debt? MODERATE. Calculated from the cash flow statement, the company's debt-to-equity ratio in the previous quarter was 1.6. Its peer companies average 1.7.
- How well is the company positioned to withstand an economic downturn? IT MUST CONTINUE TO LOWER ITS DEBT AND INCREASE ITS OPERATING MARGIN TO ADEQUATELY WITHSTAND AN ECONOMIC DOWNTURN.
- How does the company compare with other industry competitors? ABOUT AVERAGE TO ITS PEER GROUP.

Correct answers to the business language quiz on page 19: 1—B; 2—A; 3—D; 4—F; 5—E; 6—G; 7—C.

Chapter 3

Building the Business Case for Learning

What's in this chapter:

- How to create a business-focused value proposition statement for your learning function.
- How to formulate an annual learning plan for your organization.
- How to develop a powerful business case that will enable you to get the funding for your learning project.

■ ■ ■

Business leaders must make decisions on a host of issues, such as which projects to fund, which suppliers to use, and which products to bring to market. Business cases are commonly used decision-making tools used to help leaders assess the viability of a proposed investment or project. A business case provides the justification for an investment or project. Ultimately, it is "building the case" for management's commitment and approval.

As a learning leader, you have many opportunities to build and reinforce the business case for investing and supporting learning. To ensure alignment between learning and your stakeholders, they must see why and how learning contributes to their overall business success. That is the focus of this chapter—step 2 of the Strategic Learning Alignment Model: *Building the Business Case for Learning*. You will be able to leverage the work from step 1, *Knowing Your Business*, to help you build a strong business case for the learning function and your learning solutions.

This chapter focuses on three key activities to drive understanding of why the learning function is critical to creating value for the business:

- Creating a clear and specific value proposition. This brief but well-crafted message explains why your learning function exists within your company. Your value proposition should directly align with and drive the business strategy.
- Formulating your annual learning plan through business leadership engagement and sponsorship.
- Developing value-added business cases for specific project investments.

The systematic use of all three of these activities powers the "business case" for learning and results in strong alignment between learning and your business.

Using Value Proposition Statements

Business leaders use value proposition statements to communicate how the company's products or services add value to a targeted set of customers. These brief, definitive statements should capture both the minds and hearts of customers in answering the customer's question "Why should I buy from you?" A value proposition provides the basis for branding, products or services, and marketing communications.

A value proposition is different from a company's vision or mission. The value proposition is focused on motivating a customer to choose a specific company over its competitors. For example, here is the UPS value proposition statement found on the company's website:

> UPS (United Parcel Services—the world's largest package delivery company and a leading provider of logistics services delivery). Our integrated global ground and air network is the most extensive in the industry. It is the only network that handles all levels of service (express, ground, domestic,

> international, commercial, residential) through one integrated pickup and delivery service system. Our broad portfolio of services enables customers to choose the delivery option that is most appropriate for their requirements.

This UPS value proposition is customer-centric, reflecting a wide range of products or services that meet specific customer needs in a way that differentiates the company from its competitors.

For your learning function, your business leaders' funding and support equates to their "buying" your learning solutions. If you surveyed your learning team and stakeholders today, would your value proposition roll off their tongues? Could they readily answer the question "What value does the learning function provide the business?" When learning is tightly aligned with the business's priorities, both the learning team and stakeholders can readily articulate the learning function's value proposition.

The value proposition is the framework from which your learning function should consistently operate. As with a business value proposition statement, it provides the basis for your branding, solutions, and communication. It reflects your understanding of the business and its strategy. It also provides a clear purpose for the learning team, guiding their communications and actions.

Creating Your Learning Value Proposition Statement

Even though a value proposition statement is only a few sentences long, it does require time and thought to create. The framework given in figure 3-1 can serve as a guide for creating your value proposition statement, which should contain these five components:

- business objective
- learning solutions
- value
- proof
- differentiation.

Figure 3-1. A Framework for Creating Your Value Proposition Statement

Component	Business Leader Viewpoint	Learning Function Questions
1. Customer objective	Understand my business issues and goals.	What business issue are you solving for your business leaders?
2. Learning solutions	Tell me how you are going to help me.	What do you provide to help your business address these issues and goals?
3. Value	Tell me how this will benefit me.	What unique value do your learning solutions provide your business leaders?
4. Proof	Tell me why I should believe this.	What data do we have that proves we can deliver this value to our business leaders?
5. Differentiation	Tell me how you are uniquely positioned to do this for me.	How does our learning solution differ from other potential competitors?

As tempting as it is to begin with your learning solutions—of which you are knowledgeable and proud—the starting point is to examine business strategy and stakeholder needs. Follow these steps:

- On a blank piece of paper, list the strategic business issues facing your stakeholders.
- List the learning solutions you offer to help your business leaders address these issues. Your solution should tie directly to solving the business issue.
- List how the learning solution you provide adds value to the business leaders. Think beyond learning "product" and view your total learning solution. For example, you may have solid learning content, but you may also add value in your use of action learning to address real business issues and your use of leaders as teachers (see chapter 4).

Anyone can promise to deliver value. However, what proof points support your claim to deliver value and are also important to your stakeholders? Cost, quality, and time factors are typically important to business leaders and are potential proof points for each of these factors:

- Cost—do you leverage global learning suppliers to drive the affordable, local delivery of learning?
- Quality—do you engage leaders as teachers to ensure that learning is business relevant?
- Time—does your learning function have the track record of producing rapid, just-in-time learning solutions to accelerate competitive capabilities?

Your comparative knowledge of other learning options and solutions available to your business leaders will help you determine why you are the preferred learning supplier. For example, business leaders have choices to create leadership education within their business units or use externals sources. Your differentiation could be your ability to obtain economies of scale by providing a global solution (cost) and company-wide consistency (quality).

Take your completed list and discuss it with a representative sample of your key business stakeholders, who are your best resource to find out what value you bring. Some of us shy away from directly asking this question of our stakeholders. If your list aligns with your stakeholders' view of learning, then you have important validation. But if your list is not aligned with their view, you have a timely opportunity to refine your value proposition statement. The process of discussing your value proposition with your stakeholders actually engages them and drives alignment.

Finally, apply the "Business leader—'So what?' test" to your value proposition to ensure that you are communicating tangible, business-centric value. For example, "Our learning group reaches more than 20,000 participants each year." So what? Why is this important to your business stakeholders? This may lead you to alter your statement to read "We use high quality global instructors to reach more than 20,000 participants each year." This provides more of a business-centric view of value. However, again ask "So what?" What is the distinct value for the business leader? Your next iteration might read "We bring locally delivered, consistent, quality learning to your employees in every country where you operate your business." This last statement conveys minimal travel expenses, accessibility to learning across the globe, and the assurance that there is a consistent level of quality regardless of the geographic offering.

Figure 3-2 depicts a strong value proposition for a learning function. This value proposition statement is a powerful tool for creating business leader alignment, as well as learning team alignment. It provides the foundation from which you operate your learning function.

Formulating Your Annual Learning Plan

Another important aspect of building the case for learning is the formulation of your Annual Learning Plan. The process of creating the ALP presents an opportunity to engage stakeholders and align to the company's annual business planning processes. A simple fact of life is that rarely are there enough resources to provide all the strategic learning that

Figure 3-2. A Strong Value Proposition for a Learning Function

Component	Business Leader Viewpoint	Value Proposition for Learning
1. Business objective	Understand my business issues and goals.	To support our company's growth in emerging markets,
2. Learning solutions	Tell me how you are going to help me.	We provide global, accelerated development programs.
3. Value	Tell me how this will benefit me.	What data do we have that quickly close skill gaps for employees in these markets.
4. Proof	Tell me why I should believe this.	On average, business leaders estimate our accelerated development programs decrease learning time by more than 20 percent.
5. Differentiation	Tell me how you are uniquely positioned to do this for me.	We accomplish this by using customized, real-world business simulations in all our learning.

is requested across your company. Given this reality, it is critical to engage your business leaders in learning governance to validate your learning priorities (see more on this in chapter 4), approve funding, and sponsor your ALP. This ensures the alignment of learning with the business's goals and clarity on your annual deliverables.

Figure 3-3 illustrates the engagement of multitude sources of strategic input, the key learning activities to create the ALP, and the ALP's process alignment with the annual business-planning calendar. These sources of input include

- strategic business plans
- annual talent and organizational capability review
- performance management system
- learning college advisory councils
- enterprise learning leader councils
- external best practice learning benchmarking
- functional learning plans for applicable business units.

Using multiple sources of strategic input engages your key stakeholders in the planning process. In addition to your reviewing the business plans and capability assessments, the dialogue with your stakeholders on their learning needs is invaluable. You have an opportunity to share your knowledge of their business and gain a deeper understanding of the learning implications of their strategy. Compiling and communicating an analysis of strategic learning needs builds your transparency with the business, fostering increased alignment with its goals. Thus, your ALP needs to be derived from an open analysis of data and to be openly approved by a cross-section of senior executives. Depending on the size and structure of your organization, business unit and functional-level business plans can be compiled and then reflected in the company's overall ALP.

Typically, your business unit human resource colleagues play a major role in helping you understand the business strategy and learning needs at their business unit level. In addition to learning needs input, key human resource leaders should also have a role in the final approval of your ALP. When followed by broad communication of your ALP,

Figure 3-3. Annual Learning Plan Intake and Prioritization Approval Process

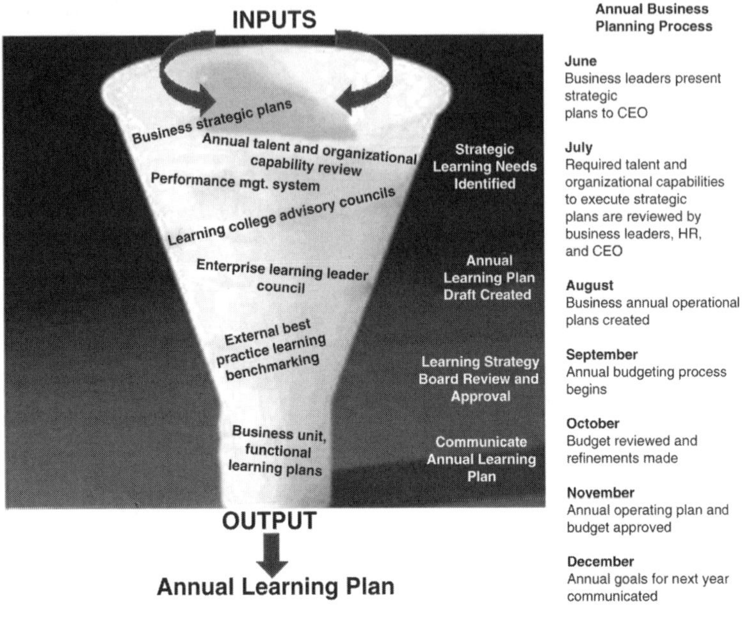

the inclusiveness and openness of your process minimizes questioning about why and how the learning function selected certain learning priorities.

Keep in mind that your ALP should leverage the processes, tools, and language of your business. When you approach your plan from this business-centric view, you increase your credibility and alignment with the business leaders. Your ALP needs to include these key components:

- Common strategic learning themes, which describe the learning competency needed, such as strategic marketing skills.
- A skills gap description, which provides detail on the specific competency gap, such as identifying unmet customers needs.
- Targeted audience penetration goals, which identify the roles and numbers of people you plan to reach with your learning solution. For example, a strategic marketing learning solution audience is product manager leadership. The total number of product

manager leaders is 100. In the first year, you expect to reach 75 participants with your strategic marketing learning solution.

- Prioritized learning themes, which represent the rank order of your strategic learning themes. For example, your first priority is strategic marketing, and your second priority is channel development.
- Existing and new learning solutions to address the skills gap, which identify learning solutions that could address the skills gap—for example, a new program, Workshop on Strategic Marketing for Innovation, and an existing program, Strategic Competitive Analysis.
- The organizational capacity to consume learning solutions, which summarize the potential time impact of learning solutions on different target audiences. For example, sales managers will average three and a half days of formal learning each year.
- A choice of investment options, which is a menu of incremental investment levels and corresponding learning solutions. For example, choice A—with a $200,000 budget—delivers nine programs for senior-level manager learning; choice B—with a $250,000 budget—delivers nine programs for senior-level managers plus five coaching workshops; and choice C—with a $300,000 budget—delivers nine programs for senior-level managers plus five coaching workshops, as well as the refreshment of existing marketing learning programs.
- An impact measurement plan, which provides a schedule, target learning programs, and the evaluation methods you will use. For example, in the months June–July 2012, strategic marketing programs, evaluated with participant and management surveys and interviews.

Figure 3-4 is an excerpt from an annual learning plan created by a corporate university. This matrix is the output of learning needs identification and analysis. It visually shows the common strategic learning priorities for the four sectors of the overall business. A brief description of the skills gap follows. The target audience is identified, along with learning solution penetration goals for the coming year. For example, approximately 100 product managers across the globe constitute the target audience for a strategic marketing learning solution. However, the ALP indicates that 75 product managers will actually receive the learning solution in the upcoming year.

In this case, their managers must carefully prioritize the selection of product managers to participate in the learning workshop. The penetration goals are a balance of the amount of learning resources, the business organization's capacity to consume the learning, and the criticality of the skills gap. The final column of figure 3-4 indicates the corresponding learning solutions that are recommended. Note that this matrix does not contain funding implications.

Some practitioners (including me) prefer to use a matrix similar to the one shown in figure 3-5 as a basis for a strategic learning need prioritization discussion. First, determine if the strategic learning needs are aligned with the priorities of business leaders. Then discuss the funding required. Of course, there are also a number of other effective ways to construct an ALP. It could include an executive summary and a matrix that does include key investment data—the percentage of total investment, volume, and per person cost ranges. The format you choose should align with the metrics valued within your organization. For instance, the ALP for a company that places a strong emphasis on volume metrics could include the number of deliveries and participants, along with a matrix giving year-over-year increases.

Figure 3-6 represents an ALP executive summary. The company for which this ALP was created focuses heavily on running relatively flat budgets and demonstrating year-over-year productivity gains. In other words, it seeks to continue to work smarter and deliver more with the same amount of investment. Its business leaders are held accountable for productivity metrics. It is logical that the learning function should operate in the same way to be truly aligned with the business's goals.

Another key component of your ALP is an analysis of the organization's capacity to consume the learning solutions you propose (see figure 3-7). I have seen talented learning professionals create robust learning

Figure 3-4. An Excerpt from an Annual Learning Plan

Common Strategic Learning Priorities: Target Audience and Solutions

Learning Need	Sector #1	Sector #2	Sector #3	Sector #4	Skill Gap	Targeted Audience (total/annual goal)	Learning Solution
Strategic Marketing*	■	■	■	■	• Identifying unmet customer needs • Developing pricing/promotion plans per segment	Product Mgt Leaders [100/75]	Strategic Marketing for Innovation workshop [new] Executive Mentor Program [new]
Channel Development*	■	■	■	■	• Evaluating channel profitability • Driving growth thru channel programs	Regional Sales Managers [150/150]	New online program [available now] Action learning regional projects [new]
Change Leadership*	■	■	■	■	• Creating a culture of change • Leader's role in sustaining change	Major initiatives change leaders [20/20]	Change Leadership Workshop Action learning change initiative projects [new]
General Mgt*	■	■	■	■	• Running a service business	New Service Managers [34/34]	Service Academy [available now] Action learning projects [new]
Globalization				■	• Understanding how to do business in other cultures	High potential Mid-Level Managers [300/100]	External Partnership Program with Thunderbird [new]
Matrix Management			■	■	• Influencing across organizations • Collaboration	HiPo Ops Mgrs [60/20]	Rotational assignments coaching [available now]
Customer Service		■	■		• Service culture • Individual's role in delivering quality service	Sales and Service Assoc. [3000/3000]	Online customized program [available now]
Lean Six Sigma Manufacturing	■				• Applied lean Black Belt skills	Plant Managers [80/20]	Sector-Deployed Lean Six Sigma BB Certification [available now]

■ = Identified as Priority Need by BU   * = Common Strategic Priority for Sector

plans that omit this step. While these professionals are presenting their ALP, the business leaders then ask this fundamental question: "What is the impact of your plan on employee time away from the job?"

The capacity to consume data shows your understanding of the business and your effort to keep aligned with the "learning tolerance threshold" of your organization. Here the metric of a "learning day" is helpful. The average learning day's calculation per key role includes formal learning activities and converts this into a learning day. For example, a learning day could be made up of three hours of online learning and

Figure 3-5. A Sample Targeted Approach for a Strategic Learning Need Prioritization Discussion

Priorities for 2012 Enterprise Learning Plan

Learning solutions that increase OI (operational income), develop bench strength, and drive revenue were prioritized first:

- Operations
- Leadership–focus on Business Leadership
- Sales

(These three priority areas represents 67% of the total learning plan investment)

Learning solutions in the following areas were also prioritized for developing strategic competencies:

- Strategic Marketing
- People Skills to Drive Talent Stewardship
- Service

Given these priorities, the investment for general studies shifts from classroom offerings to online offerings, expanding the learning and development opportunities available for employees.

2012 Enterprise Learning Plan is prioritized for highest impact on short-term results (operations and sales) and long-term business strategy (leadership).

Proposed 2012 Enterprise Learning Plan

	Investment (% of Total)	**# of Deliveries (classroom)**	**# of Participants**	**Cost Per Participant (range)**
OpEx 1 Online	24	61	1582 1000	$400-700; Black Belt, Supply Chain $1600 $5
Leadership	23	18	504	Senior leader $6300; Mid-level leader $3000 Leader $1800; Front-line supervisor $300
Sales 4 Online	20	22	550 10500	$700-1800 Solution Selling $5-65 Selling to Vertical Markets
People Skills to Talent Stewardship 2 Online	14	57	1420 1500	$300-700 $5
General Studies *SkillSoft Online*	12	6	117 4000	$500-750 $58
Marketing	5	4	108	$1500-1800 Marketing for Innovation
Service	2	10	200	$250 Leading a Service Business
Totals	**100%**	**178** (14% increase v '11)	**4,480 classroom** (26% increase v '11) **17,000 online**	

Figure 3-6. A Sample Executive Summary for an Annual Learning Plan

2012 Learning Plan Funding—Corporate University:

Executive Summary

Our Corporate University's mission to deliver strategic learning that is "common, core, and critical" for the enterprise is unchanged. In support of transformational change occurring within the Company, however, Corporate University's scope continues to expand to serving all Corporate University employees with a broader portfolio of learning programs and services.

Business drivers for Corporate University's expansion include Enterprise Focus Area (EFA) initiatives, Company's compliance standards/requirements, top line growth through solution selling, basic skill gaps in emerging markets, employee engagement survey results calling for increasing employee training opportunities, supply chain opportunities, and opportunities to leverage enterprise learning resources.

In creating this 2012 Funding Plan, the Corporate University removed more than $500,000 in variable costs. In addition, we forecasted a 10% productivity increase administration training in business University Corporate and management. In 2012, recurring year-over-year (YOY) savings from the 2011 vendor optimization initiative allows Corporate University to deliver an additional 23% of basic business programs with a flat budget.

Key highlights of the 2012 Corporate University Learning Plan Funding:

- No increase in FTE (staff)
- 2% increase over 2011 budget. However, half of this increase is one-time expense for expansion of users for our learning management system.
- Incremental Corporate University deliverables and services include:
  - **>70% YOY increase in delivery of EFA learning programs (includes development of 8 new programs).** Current 2012 EFA training requests are in excess of 30 new programs and 76 additional deliveries. This amount of training is not feasible for the Company organization to consume. Based on our capacity to consume analysis and EFA leadership prioritization, the Corporate University Learning Funding Plan reflects a reduced and more practical number of new programs and deliveries.
  - **Initial implementation of learning technology to distribute all training programs globally and accelerate EFA training deployment.** Corporate University's global reach to a wider target audience and potential for an expanding employee base via acquisition and the increasing Company's compliance standards/requirements drive a modest (1% of total Plan) one-time investment of learning technology in 2012. Benchmarked companies typically deliver 30% of training via learning technology and experience rapid, expanded training penetration, as well as reduction in training costs. We are currently at 15% level.
  - **>80% YOY increase in delivery of Corporate University College programs thru launch of Sales and OPEX (Operational Excellence) Colleges** (Sales-36 deliveries, 2 new programs developed and OPEX-3 deliveries of new programs, 1 new program developed).
  - **Leverage of overall Company training spend via launch of Enterprise Learning Services.** A *conservative* estimate of the Company enterprise spend on internal and external training is in excess of $30M. This investment is completely under-leveraged. Typical results from leveraging an enterprise training spend results in a 10-20% reduction of the spend. Corporate University needs to lead this effort in 2012 with the implementation of an Enterprise Learning Services strategy. We estimate delivering a synergy save of $3M.
  - **Continued brokered-managed services support of training for the emerging markets.** These Corporate University services address the need for basic skill training in emerging markets, without adding the General Administration burden of a training infrastructure for each growing business. It also allows leverage of the enterprise economies of scale and scalability for acquisitions. In 2011, more than 700 Company employees in ESA and China will attend these programs. In addition, the managed services Corporate University provides for Course-On-Location will touch an additional 750 employees.

four hours of a learning lab. Of course, informal learning time may also be factored in.

The purpose of the capacity-to-consume analysis is to provide directional data on the time impact of your learning plan. Emphasize the approximate and directional nature of the data. Seek a consensus among the business leaders on the maximum number of learning days they are willing to allot. This will provide you with a guideline as you finalize and execute your ALP.

Figure 3-7 illustrates a "menu choice" approach to obtaining funding for your ALP that corresponds to the ALP executive summary in figure 3-6. Remember, multiple departments are competing for funding from the company's annual budget. As business leaders are forced to make tough funding choices, it is important to align their choice with the corresponding learning solutions delivered. Many times, a smaller funding amount is approved, but business leaders do not fully understand the impact of this decrease. You leave the meeting room with two different sets of expectations for annual deliverables. It is important that your business leaders are completely educated consumers who fully understand the impact of their funding decisions. You need to provide them with funding level choices that have clear deliverables associated with each funding-level. Use this as an opportunity to align with your business leaders' goals and share accountability for the ALP.

Figure 3-8 shows different levels of investment and what each level "buys" in learning solution deliverables. This menu choice provides transparent data from which the business leaders can select their preferred level of investment. It also reinforces the alignment of expectations between the learning function and business leaders' priorities. Opportunities and risks are included for each level of investment.

The final component of your ALP is a high-level plan of how you intend to measure the impact of your learning solutions. Figure 3-9 shows an impact measurement plan with targeted learning solutions, evaluation methodology, and timeframes. In your ALP process, you are requesting funds from a limited pool, literally at the expense of another company department. You absolutely should include your plan to capture impact metrics in the overall ALP.

Figure 3-7. The "Menu Choice" Approach to Obtaining Funding for Your Annual Learning Plan

2012 Learning Plan Organizational Capacity to Consume

Target Population	# of Courses Available	Average Courses Per Person*	Typical Training Days
Managers (2,000)	36	4	9
Individual Contributors (14,000)	29	1	3.5
Supervisors (700)	3	1	3.5
Sales Managers (500)	16	4	9
Sales (1,770)	13	1	3.5
Marketing (675)	15	1	3.5
Supply Chain Managers (300)	15	4	9
Technicians (1120)	13	1	3.5
Quality Managers (200)	11	5	9
Quality (700)	11	1	3.5

* Based on seats available and assumes mix of online and instructor-led programs

2012 Learning Plan Organizational Capacity to Consume: People Managers

Target Population	Total Potential Reach # of People	# of Courses Available	Average Courses Per Person	Total Training Days*
Managers (2,000)	**7718**	**36**	**4**	**9**

Available Programs	
Advanced Leader Business Mgmt Advanced Leader People Mgmt Leader People Management Sales Effectiveness & Productivity Solution Sales Advanced Pricing Driving Dramatic Growth Marketing for the IR Manager Business Acumen Team Leadership Interpersonal Leadership Project Management Roadmap for Change IR Orientation Ideas to Action Lean Fundamentals LSS Leader LSS Sr. Leader Green Belt Black Belt Productivity Tool box Productivity Overview Supplier Development Toolbox Logistics Toolbox Quality Leadership	SIOP Awareness CEM Cultural Awareness New Market Entry BOS Module CSI & Customer Metrics Service Contracts Extended Warranty Coaching for Performance Coaching Fundamentals Talent Stewardship Competency Based Assessment Value Innovation & Contextual Interviewing

***Based on seats available and assumes mix of online and instructor-led programs**

Course Examples	Training Days
LSSL	2
ALBM	4
CEM	2
Coaching Fundamentals-(online)	½
Talent Stewardship-(online)	½
TOTAL	9

Although the ALP content is now complete, your process is not. Communicating this plan to your stakeholders is the critical next step. As the year progresses, new strategic learning needs may arise. If so, you need a systematic process to evaluate them in the context of your ALP and to determine what resources need to be shifted or increased to include them. As these requests arise, it is wise to have the senior-

Figure 3-8. "Menu Choice" of Learning Investments: Different Levels of Investment and What Each Level "Buys" in Learning Solutions

	Base Budget + Ongoing Delivery of 2011 Existing Programs	Strategic Corporate University Initiatives	New EFA Training Request Initiatives
	• Leadership & GM (11) • Core (32) • Emerging Mkt. Management Services Programs (21) • Marketing (5) • Course-On-Location (20) • Leadership Forum (3) • Leadership Conference (1) • Refresh Marketing Programs (2) • EFA Programs (45)	• Launch Sales College (36 programs delivered and 2 developed) • Launch OPEX College (3 programs delivered and 1 developed) • Develop Company Orientation program • Initial implementation of learning technology to distribute learning • Launch Enterprise Learning Services to leverage Company training spend (deliver $3M synergy saves in 2012)	• Deliver 19 new EFA programs • Develop 8 new EFA programs
Deliverables	**Opportunity With This Level of Investment:** Continuation of 3 year learning delivery plan **Risk With This Level Investment:** No new program development No launch of Sales or OPEX Colleges No new EFA training programs developed No implementation of learning technology to distribute learning No Enterprise Learning Services to leverage Company training spend.	**Opportunity With Incremental Level of Investment:** 80% YOY increases in Sales and OPEX programs $3M synergy saves **Risk With This Level Investment:** No Company Orientation program to address major merger activity No Sales and OPEX programs No realization of $3M synergy saves	**Opportunity With Incremental Level of Investment:** 70% YOY increase in EFA programs **Risk With This Level Investment:** No additional EFA programs
	$6.9M + **Base Funding Level**	**$3.3 M = $10.2 M** + **New Funding to Support 2012 Learning Plan**	**$200K = $10.4 M* 2% Increase Over 2011 Budget* Recommendation**

Figure 3-9. A Sample Impact Measurement Plan

2012 Business Impact-Level Evaluation Schedule and Methodology

Key Priority Program	Schedule									
	Apr	May	Jun	Jul	Aug	Sep	Oct	Nov	Dec	
Strategic Marketing (Q1) • Participant estimate of program value • Manager estimate of program value • Leadership assessment of improved quality of marketing plans			Survey/Interview					Survey/Interview		
Channel Development (Q2) • Channel Profitability Improvements									Pre-Post Study	
ABLM (Q1) (advanced business leader mgt) • Sample group mini- 360 degree feedback results on business results and people leadership components						Mini 360 feedback				
Change Leadership (Q2-Q4) • Sample group mini- 360 degree feedback results on change leadership									Mini 360 feedback	
Customer Service Online (Q1-Q4) • 100% Utilization Goal Met • Participant and Manager Value Estimate								Survey/Interview		

level sponsor work with you to create a business case to present to your learning governance for approval. The rigor to this process in creating a business case and presenting it to executive-level leaders for approval tends to weed out less strategically important requests. The senior-level sponsor should present the learning request, with the staff involved in the learning function playing a support role. Create a system for monthly or quarterly reviews of new strategic learning requests by your learning governance leaders. This will ensure that you maintain an ongoing transparency in the learning request process. In addition, decisions to shift or increase resources need to be shared between business leaders and learning professionals to prevent misalignment between your deliverables and corresponding resources.

As you can see, there are two key factors to your ALP—one is process and the other is content. Both factors must be business-centric to ensure that you are aligned with the strategic needs of your organization and are following the business-planning cadence. This business-centric approach enables you to build a business case for learning. In the process, it also drives your credibility and alignment with business leaders' goals.

Developing a Business Case to Fund a Learning Project

Part of developing the business case for learning can literally include building a case to request funding for a learning project. A business case provides potential investors with information on why investing in your project is a good decision. Investors look to see a return on their investment. The concept of return on investment is no different for learning leaders requesting funding. Most business cases provide decision makers with a similar format of information, helping them compare multiple case requests. The research and analysis incorporated into a business case can be referred to as "due diligence."

Typically, business cases are written for nonroutine and more costly investments—for instance, the purchase of million-dollar production equipment or an investment in a company software platform. Your company will have policies regarding the requirement for a business case. Regardless of the requirement, the process of completing a business case provides value for your learning team. It reinforces a business-centric approach and requires business rigor as learning professionals perform their due diligence.

The most common components of a business case include

- a brief description of the project
- a description of the business issue(s) resolved by the investment
- a data on benefits of the project
- a description of alternatives
- the investment requested
- an estimation of project returns/benefits.

Figure 3-10 provides a sample excerpt from a business case for a capital expenditure to create a leadership learning lab facility. The facility will decrease costs to conference centers and literally pay for itself in six months.

This business case example opens with a brief description of the project, followed by an explanation of how the business problem will be solved through meeting this request. Additional data on the benefits of the leadership learning lab appears next. The next component is a description of alternatives. This business case closes with investment requirements and payback data. Detailed data on costs and cost savings is included in the addendums to the business case.

Figure 3-10. A Sample Excerpt from a Business Case for a Capital Expenditure to Create a Leadership Learning Laboratory

Year One Cost Savings

			Per Day Expenses including taxes and service chg							
	Location	Per Person	Sleeping Room Cost**	Catering*	Total Cost Per Day	# of Days	Sub-total	Extra Dinner Misc. Chgs.	A/V per session	TOTAL
Top Gun Academy	Lodge	35	6,583.00	3,255.00	9,838.00	9	88,542.00	2,000.00	2,500.00	93,042.00
Top Gun Academy	Corp U	35	2,304.00	1,750.00	4,054.00	9	36,486.00	2,000.00	N/C	38,486.00
									Savings per two session program	54,556.00
Sleeping Room Costs									X	4
Lodge	195.80								**Total Savings**	218,224

*Catering package includes breakfast, breaks, lunch, and 1 dinner

Year Two Cost Savings

Senior Leader Programs	# Programs	Savings Per Day	Days Per Program	Total Savings Per Program	Total Savings Per Offering
Top Gun Academy	3	$6,000	9	$54,000	$162,000
Leader Level - People Mgmt	4	$6,000	4	$21,000	$84,000
Advanced Leader - People Mgmt	3	$6,000	4	$24,000	$72,000
Advanced Leader - Business Management	3	$6,000	4	$24,000	$72,000
Strategic Planning	3	$6,000	2	$12,000	$36,000
Strategic Change	2	$6,000	3	$18,000	$36,000
Total Savings Per Year					$462,000

Another example of a business case appears in figure 3-11. This example reflects a purchase order request for the design and pilot delivery of a new sales learning program. In the right margin, boxed descriptors are added to help you identify the business-centric elements. As you scan through figure 3-11, note the business sponsorship and "pull" for this program. Benefits are stated in business terms. Business leaders are concerned with the shelf life, or life cycle, of their products. They focus on the products' growth, maturity, and decline. Similarly, the life cycle of this learning investment is of interest to business leaders. In this case example, the learning program is viable for three years without major revisions.

Additional quantitative data appears in the next sections of this business case, including target audience penetration targets, itemized costs, and unit costs. These numbers are familiar data points for business leaders. External alternative sales learning programs are referenced for comparison purposes. Finally, the vendor selection process highlights the engagement of the company's procurement expertise, and business leaders select the vendor.

The business language and metrics used in this business case mirror the rigor that business leaders use when they request funds. By replicating a rigorous business approach, you can ensure that your business case will be received with greater credibility and the likelihood of approval.

Presenting Your Business Case for Approval

After building your initial case, you will likely need to present it to business leaders to gain approval. It is wise to have a financial colleague, as well as the project sponsor, review your business case before you present it to business leaders. You do not want a misused or weak financial metric to derail your presentation. Senior business leaders are quite fluent in financial metrics—the language of business. Therefore, it is highly probable you be will challenged on a misused or weak financial metric. The time for correction or omission of the data is during your review with your finance colleague and project sponsor.

Prepare for your presentation by thinking about the questions you are likely to hear, for example:

Figure 3-11. An Example of a Business Case for a Purchase Order Request for a New Sales Learning Program

Requisition #: 12345

Creation Date: February 18, 2008

Payee: **Company X**

Amount $$$: **$94,500**

Requested by: **Business Sponsor** and Chief Learning Officer

Business Sponsorship

Originated by: Sr. Manager, Sales & Marketing Education

Chargeback to BU/Sector?: ☐Y☐ N   Approved in AOP?: ☐Y☐ N   Aligned with Corp Tech Strategy?: ☐Y☐ N

Description of Requisition: Contract for Development and Pilot of Sales College "Solution Sales" Program

Upfront Alignment and "Pull" from the Business

This requisition is for the development and pilot of the **"Solution Sales"** program. This is the second program in the suite of 3 "Solution Sales" programs to be developed by Corporate Univesityin support of **the enterprise-wide sales training strategy approved by the Sales & Marketing College Advisory Council.** Company X will provide customized curriculum development and delivery of this program in 2008.

Business-centric Benefits

The enterprise benefits of this program are (1) Consistent solution sales methodology and documented sales processes across the enterprise, (2) Increased revenue from non-product services and recurring revenue opportunities, (3) Increased volume and gross profit of goods sold by leveraging financial acumen skills to document solutions impact on customers P&L, (4) Increased customer satisfaction and loyalty as a result of strategic business partner solution sales approach, and (5) Enabler in attraction/retention of talent and increased ability to transition talent across sectors and business units.

Program Description:

This is a blended, customized program made up of 3 distinct learning events: (1) Pre-work will consist of one e-learning module on the basics of Financial Acumen (including assessment) and one pre-work activity based on an actual customer account. A manager's guide book and coaching tips to promote manager/participant goal setting and program expectations will also be included. (2) A classroom module (3 days) of skill-based practice, application, role play and feedback based on learning specifications developed by the IR global cross-sector design team and aligned with IR sales competencies. (3) Post-work, which includes interactive salesperson/manager 30, 60, 90 day goal follow-up program to drive adoption and implementation of specific goals set at the conclusion of the 3 day program.

Participants will leave with tools and templates that can be applied to daily work assignments, including pre-call planning, customer presentations, and customer proposals. **Shelf-life for this program is 3 years.**

The objective of this program is for sales professionals to maximize their sales performance metrics by

- Partnering with customers to uncover and understand customer challenges, objectives and initiatives
- Targeting customer solutions that focus on "value" as articulated by the customer, versus focusing on a specific product
- Developing customer solutions based on the "Value Framework" process focusing on business outcomes, required capabilities, measurement, value differentiation and proof points
- Using business acumen to quantify and dollarize solution savings by identifying how the IR solution impacts the customers P&L
- Leveraging value via key customer relationships and demonstrated value of Ingersoll Rand

Target Audience:

The target audience for this program is approximately X number of outside territory sales professional's enterprise wide and X number of frontline sales managers. Managers will determine nominations for this program by (1) prioritizing sales professionals that have completed Sales Effectiveness & Productivity, (2) top performing sales professionals that were exempt from Sales Effectiveness based on performance and, (3) all frontline sales managers. We will deliver 14 programs in 2008 and 20 deliveries per year in 2009, 2010, and 2011 to **achieve penetration rates above 90% for sales professionals and frontline sales managers.**

Audience Penetration Targets

Development and Delivery Schedule and Financial Impact:

The **"Solution Sales"** program will be designed and developed according to the following schedule.

One-time development fees and delivery of pilot:

Milestone	Conclusion Date	Fees
Custom program development	6/15/08	$
E-learning module development	6/15/08	$
Pilot	7/7/08	$
After action review	7/14/08	Included
Final curriculum, facilitator/participant guides, pre/post work materials	7/21/08	Included
Total amount		$94,500

Itemized Costs

Unit Cost

The **cost per participant day for the "Solution Sales" program is $153 including meals and materials.** Similar sales programs offered through franchised sales training companies (listed here) average **$385** per participant day. University sponsored corporate education courses (listed here) average **$1,400** per participant day.

External Benchmark Comparisons

A design team consisting of 18 company business leaders, representing all 3 sectors and the regions of Asia, Americas, and Europe was assembled per the Corporate University Phase Gate process. The Solution Sales Executive Program Sponsor and all design team members approved the learning specifications and objectives outlined for this program.

Procurement Expertise Is Leveraged

Vendor Selection

Corporate University followed its standard Phase Gate Process and worked with **Strategic Sourcing.** A full RFP was sent to 10 vendors in September 2007. An updated RFI - RFP was sent in January 2008 to the 3 vendors that best fit the company requirements of sales expertise and qualifications, global experience and delivery capabilities, and service delivery approach and financial impact.

Business Leaders Select Vendor

The top 2 vendors were provided the opportunity to present their formal proposals to the Sales College Design Team. Both vendor presentations were scored using a standard scoring matrix and prescribed scoring anchors.

By unanimous decision, **the business leader design team and Corporate University chose to partner with Company X** due to its demonstrated abilities and service delivery approach. Company X will work with the Sales College Design Team components in the development of this program ensuring alignment of existing sales methodologies, tools and processes. Company X has completed similar work with other Fortune 500 companies. Company X also ranked as the **low cost provider (15% less)** based on RFP and proposal results. Payment terms are Net 60 days.

Negotiated Low Cost Provider for Targeted Level of Quality

Contact Information Company X;

Summary and Wrap Up

The **"Solution Sales"** program is part of the Enterprise Sales Training Strategy developed by the Corporate University Sales College Advisory Council. This program is aligned with the company vision and will be a strategic enabler in Driving Dramatic Growth, Operational Excellence, and Dual Citizenship. This solution sales methodology and documented sales process will be reinforced by sales managers in pre and post work activities. **Company X** has an existing relationship with the Corporate University through their mutual partnership with Company Y. Company X will develop and deliver a world-class curriculum that is customized to our company's specific business requirements in direct support of our company goals and aspirations.

Approved by:

Date

- What level of usage do you expect from this new leadership learning lab?
- How do other companies address this issue?
- What is the payback period for this investment?
- What kind of discount did you negotiate with the vendor that you've recommended?
- What is the shelf life for this program?
- How long will it take you to put our entire sales force through this program?

"Presell" or share your presentation in advance with a few key members of the group to which you will be presenting. Getting their potential objections and questions before presenting to the larger group will help you prepare for and manage these potential trouble spots.

Senior business leaders want communication that is concise, clear, and ultimately answers the question "How will this generate or save me money?" Within the senior business leader group, there are differences in roles and personalities. Take the time before your presentation to complete a stakeholder analysis.

For example, a stakeholder analysis will likely indicate that the CEO and chief financial officer will want information emphasizing different focuses. Thus your CEO may be focused on increasing sales in a new global market. And although your CFO will also be aligned with this marketing focus, he or she will probably be more focused on decreasing the price discounts used by salespeople to generate more profitability in company sales. Therefore, you should frame your sales learning program business case so it's relevant to the focal points of both your CEO and CFO.

Here are some tips to follow when delivering your presentation:

- Open your presentation with a clear desired outcome. For example, "I am here to obtain funding for a learning sales program that will generate increased profitable sales for the company."
- Provide a brief description of the business issue you are addressing in your presentation.

- Highlight the benefits and return on investment for your recommendation. It is also useful to highlight the risks of not making the investment.
- Check for alignment with phrases such as " So far, is this making sense to you?" and "Am I on the right track here?" Ask for verbal responses—do not assume that silence means agreement.

If your business case is approved, clearly recap your understanding of what specifically was approved. If your business case was not approved, ask what was missing that would have made your business case stronger. However, by using due diligence in your preparation, engaging leadership sponsorship for your request, and using the language of business in your business case, you greatly improve the likelihood of approval.

Building the case for learning begins with your value proposition statement. This is your foundation. Your annual learning plan is another avenue for building the case for learning through your engagement of leaders in the process and your business-centric approach. Finally, creating an actual business is another very literal opportunity to build the case for learning. In addition to these specific opportunities, your role is to continually build the business case for learning in everything you do as a learning function.

Key Points for Value Proposition Statements

- A value proposition statement communicates how your learning function brings unique value to the business and reinforces your business case for learning.
- When both your business stakeholders and your learning team members can readily articulate the learning function's value proposition, this is an indictor that a clear and business-aligned value proposition statement is in place.
- The five key components of your value proposition statement for learning are business objective, learning solutions, value, proof, and differentiation.
- The most important component of your value proposition statement is that it is focused on business and not on the

learning function. To ensure that you have accomplished this, apply the "Business leader—'So what?' test."

Exercises for the Value Proposition Statement

- Using the template framework given in figure 3-1, create a value proposition for your learning function.
- Working with your team and/or professional colleagues, apply the "Business leader—'So what?' test" to ensure that your statement is business focused.
- Validate your value proposition statement with key stakeholders.

Key Points for Formulating Your Annual Learning Plan

- Formulating an annual learning plan presents an opportunity to engage leaders and obtain their validation of your annual priorities.
- Your ALP should be business focused, linking learning solutions to driving the business strategy.
- Include business-oriented data in your ALP, such as target audience penetration, life cycle of the learning solution, and the organization's capacity to consume the learning proposed in your ALP.
- To obtain funding for your ALP, use the "menu choice" approach, clearly communicating deliverables for each funding level. This allows your governance board to weigh alternative levels of investment and make a very informed decision. This approach also sets and aligns expectations between the learning function and business leaders.

Exercise for Formulating Your Annual Learning Plan

Using the following checklist, conduct an audit of your current learning plan to identify possible opportunities for improvement. Write a "Y" for items currently in place and an "N" for items not yet in place in your learning plan:

____ ALP process mapped to annual business planning process.
____ Process in place for governance body to validate and approve learning plan priorities.
____ ALP contains target audience penetration goals.
____ Analysis of organizational capacity to consume learning solutions is used.
____ ALP contains benchmarking data for comparative purposes.
____ Funding "menu choice" approach used to delineate set of deliverables corresponding to each level of investment.
____ Plan in place to communicate approved ALP to key stakeholders.

On the basis of your responses in the checklist above, what areas offer the greatest continuous improvement opportunities for you?

Key Points for Developing a Business Case to Fund a Learning Project

A business case provides potential investors with information on why investing in a project is a good decision:

- Business leaders routinely use business cases in their operations management.
- Developing strong business cases for learning projects is a required capability for learning professionals.
- The due diligence involved in creating a business case provides the learning team with a business-oriented framework for their project request. This strengthens the likelihood of approval.
- Business cases typically have a similar format, making it easy for decision makers to compare multiple business case requests.

- Key components of a business case include a brief description of the project, a description of the business issue(s) resolved by the investment, data on the benefits of the project, description of alternatives, the investment requested, and an estimation of project returns/benefits.

Exercise for Building a Business Case to Fund a Learning Project

Using the following guidelines, enter the key data points for your next project business case. When complete, share with a finance colleague for feedback on the strength of your data points to obtain an approval for your project request.

- Briefly describe the project for which you seek approval.
- Why is this important to the business? Which of the following business outcomes will result from your project—increased revenues, decreased costs, faster time to market, increased operational efficiency, increased market share, increased customer satisfaction and retention, increased in quality, employee retention?
- For each of the business outcomes you identified, qualitatively and quantitatively describe expected business outcomes.
- List specifically how the key benefits of your project request will drive these business outcomes.
- What other alternatives are available?
- What were your decision criteria for selecting this project versus the alternatives?
- What is the risk to the business if funding is not approved?
- What investment is required? Is this a one-time investment or recurring?
- What return will this investment generate? What is the payback period for this investment?
- What questions or concerns could arise in the approval discussion?

Chapter 4

Engaging Leaders in Key Learning Activities

What's in this chapter:

- How to govern the learning function—ensuring that the learning process is relevant to the business, aligned with business priorities, and managed in a fiscally responsible way.
- How to design and develop learning solutions that are seen as rigorously following the regular business process for developing new products.
- How to engage leaders as teachers—including teaching, co-teaching, guest speaking, and postlearning program coaching.

■ ■ ■

The theme throughout this book is how to engage business leaders in your learning activities to create strong alignment with business priorities. In previous chapters, business-centered needs analysis and business-case creation were discussed as two such leadership engagement opportunities. As you well know, there are many activities within learning functions. However, not all activities are created equal. There are a few key activities that can create tremendous value for both the business and the learning leader. You can create unprecedented levels of engagement and alignment by directly engaging your business leaders in these key activities.

In this chapter, we focus on three key learning processes that offer tremendous opportunity for value-add engagement of your stakeholders:

- Governing the learning function.
- Designing and developing effective learning solutions.
- Engaging leaders as teachers.

These three processes constitute critical touch points between learning and your business. Closely involving your leaders in all three processes will ensure the consistent relevance and alignment of your organization's learning solutions with its business goals. Together, these processes make up step 3 of the Strategic Learning Alignment Model: *Engaging Leaders in Key Learning Activities*.

Governing the Learning Function

As I have mentioned throughout this book, business leaders often complain that the learning function is removed from the business. Of course, these same business leaders fund the learning investment, which can potentially lead to a serious disconnect between business and learning. But what do these leaders want? They simply want transparency vis-à-vis their investment. They want to know:

- Is the learning relevant to the business?
- Is the learning aligned with business priorities?
- Is the learning function managing the learning operation as a fiscally responsible business process?

These are fair questions for any investor—all pointing to the potential disconnect between business and learning. Governance systems can help eliminate this disconnect. A governance system entails the use of multiple advisory boards to ensure that your learning function is transparently on the right track. And through this formal governance system, senior business leaders and other key stakeholders provide guidance and oversight for their investment in the learning function. Thus, governance provides a strong linkage between learning and business leaders. And this in turn ensures that learning is aligned with the business's strategy and priorities. This linkage enables the learning function to deliver more impact to the company, which continues to increase the learning function's credibility.

In addition, gaining such visible support for learning from senior leaders helps to position the learning function as strategically important to the business. The leaders also bring their collective business knowledge and experiences to aid in managing the learning function. When you review award-winning learning functions, you often see that a formal governance system is in place; this is a clearly a best practice among top learning organizations—which, in fact, frequently credit their success to the strength of their governance systems.

Modeling Learning Governance After Corporate Governance

Using formal governance bodies is not a new concept—it is borrowed from the world of business. Successful for-profit and nonprofit organizations typically have a board of directors. The board's members are selected on the basis of their professional knowledge and relevant experience. To provide more diversity of thought, members also come from other unrelated industries, universities, and/or associations. The perceived quality of a corporation's governance system, such as its board, can actually influence the company's share prices (what people are willing to pay for an ownership share in the company) as well as the cost of raising capital (obtaining loans and other outside investment dollars). In the article "A Board Culture of Corporate Governance," Gabrielle O'Donovan (2003) highlights the recent renewed interest in corporate governance. In part, this is due to the high profile collapses of a number of large U.S. firms, such as Enron Corporation, and the failure of their boards to properly govern the corporation.

Across different industries and companies, the Board of Directors performs a similar set of essential oversight activities, which include

- accountability
- operational effectiveness
- program service and quality

- effective controls
- adherence to enterprise priorities.

For more, see figure 4-1.

These five basic governance responsibilities can certainly be applicable to your learning governance system. In fact, by using governance systems for your learning function, you can deliver powerful alignment with business goals.

The Structure of Learning Governance

Learning governance systems can vary in their roles and responsibilities and member composition. These can range from strategic-level, CEO-led boards to advisory councils to more operational learning councils:

- A strategic-level, CEO-led board includes senior leaders from across the company and focuses on direction, policy, and prioritization of learning.

Figure 4-1. Oversight Responsibilities for a Board of Directors

1. Accountability
■ Making a commitment to deliver measurable business results
2. Operational Effectiveness
■ Driving out costs and pursuing optimal efficiency
3. Program and Service Quality
■ Making a commitment to deliver measurable business results
4. Effective Controls
■ Accounting for and controlling expenses across the enterprise
5. Adherence to Enterprise Priorities
■ Accounting for and controlling expenses across the enterprise

Source: Corporate University Xchange, "Designing the Optimal Organization Structure & Governance Model," 2009.

- Advisory councils include a mix of midlevel through senior-level leaders who provide guidance on the direction of a curriculum.
- Operational learning councils include representation from multiple training group leaders within a company and focuses on the efficiency and effectiveness of learning across the company.

The size, geographic footprint, and complexity of your organization will influence the design of your governance system. However, at minimum, all organizations should have a strategic-level advisory board and a curriculum advisory council. You want your leaders to direct and "own" the business relevance of your learning strategy and learning solutions. Figure 4-2 summarizes the various governance bodies, roles and responsibilities, and membership composition you can use in your organization.

Designing Your Governance Team's Membership

The success of your learning governance system is largely influenced by the membership composition of your governance bodies. A stakeholder analysis, such as the one reviewed in chapter 2 (see worksheet 2-2), is extremely helpful when planning your learning governance membership to provide a visual representation of key influential stakeholders.

In addition, a stakeholder analysis identifies your most passionate supporters and most resistant stakeholders. In the early stages of organizing your governance system, it is wise to include one or two resistant leaders, who naturally will be well outnumbered by passionate supporters. As these resistant leaders engage in a learning governance role, their resistance is typically converted into more constructive guidance. In addition, your passionate supporters will exert subtle peer pressure, which typically neutralizes your resistant leader.

Along with your most senior members, you may want a midlevel leader to participate in your governance system as a career development opportunity. Midlevel managers typically view interacting with the C-suite level of senior leaders as a highly desirable opportunity. Figure 4-3 provides an example of a governance membership plan. Attention is paid to membership diversity and 18-month tenure rotations. A diverse

Figure 4-2. Strategic Levels of Learning Governance

Level of Engagement: Strategic (top) → Operational (bottom)

Governance Body	Role/Responsibility	Membership
Strategy Board	• Maintain alignment with direction of company • Set learning philosophy and policies • Identify and prioritize strategic learning needs • Approve and fund annual learning plan • Ensure learning is run as a business process • Monitor impact of learning • Visible champion for learning	• 8-10 members Standing Members: • CEO (sponsor) • Senior HR leader • Learning leader Rotating Members: • Senior Business Leaders from different lines of business, functions, and geographies • External thought leader (optional) • Minimum four meetings annually
Regional Advisory Council	• Provide regional insight into the enterprise learning direction and priorities • Identify and prioritize strategic, regional needs • Monitor impact of regional learning • Visible champion for learning within the region	• 4-6 members Standing Members: • Regional president (sponsor) • Regional HR leader • Learning leader Rotating Members: • Senior business leaders from different lines of business and functions • Minimum three meetings annually
Curriculum Advisory Council	• Set direction for curriculum area of "school" • Identify and prioritize functional • learning needs • Provide direction on target audience and levels of penetration for learning • Recommend program sponsors and design team members • Assist in obtaining necessary funding • Visible champion for the curriculum	• 4-6 members Standing Members: • Functional business leader (sponsor) e.g. CFO PVP • Sales, CHRO • Learning leader Rotating Members: • Senior leaders with content expertise (diverse lines of business and geographies) • Minimum two meetings annually
Enterprise Learning Council	• Link and leverage learning synergies • Recommend enterprise learning policies and processes • Share best practices in learning • Provide input into annual enterprise learning plan • Visible champion for learning	• 10-12 learning leader members (dependent on size/number of learning groups) • Council leadership rotated annually • Minimum four meetings annually (primarily virtual meetings)

membership consists of multiple business units and geographies. Diversity also may include variety in gender, age, and race, as well as a mix of leaders representing a range of support for your learning.

Clearly, the majority of the members of your governance system should have some passion about the importance of learning to the business. However, having a few members known for lesser support of learning will add to more robust advisory discussions and typically results in

Figure 4-3. An Example of a Strategy Board Membership Plan

Role	Name	BU	Region	Q2 2010	Q3 2010	Q4 2010	Q1 2011	Q2 2011	Q3 2011	Q4 2011
CEO	Sandy Shores									
CHRO	Bob Smith		Non-rotating members							
Learning Leader	Lance Wilkins									
Business Leader 1	Darryl Win, SVP	Drill	North America						18 Months	Phyllis Sands, SVP?
Business Leader 2	Penny Lane, CIO	Function	North America			18 Months	Harry Hopps, CFO?			
Business Leader 3	Geswant Loh, SVP	Pipe	Asia	Hem Song SVP off						
Business Leader 4	Himanshu Venky, VP	Pipe	India				18 Months	Hari Dave, SVP?		
Business Leader 5	Pablo Valez, SVP	Lock	Europe						18 Months	Pierre Fonte, VP
External Thought Leader	Albert Einstein, PhD	High Impact Learning Inc.					18 Months	Dean, UNC?		

Current Member

Potential Member

Member to Rotate Off

their increased support of learning. As members rotate on and off the board, make sure that you are providing adequate orientation to the board's charter, member roles, history, and current priorities.

Building Support for Learning Governance

Your organization may have strong C-suite support and engagement for learning, making governance relatively straightforward to implement. However, many organizations are not this fortunate. If your organization resembles the latter, here are a few strategies to drive learning governance.

The first strategy is to use your stakeholder analysis to identify your most senior passionate supporters. Approach them to serve as a steering committee. Then, with stakeholder analysis, present their participation on the steering committee as a way to address the issues and concerns that are so important to them. Be prepared to discuss their roles and responsibilities, and specify the estimated time commitment that this will involve.

Another strategy is to engage the chief financial officer in helping you ensure the company's investment in learning is getting a return. By engaging the CFO, he or she gains insight into the learning investment and can help direct spending to strategic priorities, and also becomes intimate with your process of engaging business leaders to ensure your learning is business relevant. The other business leaders will advocate your learning to the CFO, increasing his or her confidence that your learning is mission-critical to the organization.

You can even leverage your CFO as a sponsor for evaluation studies. Your key recruiting point for senior leaders is for leadership engagement to keep the learning investment aligned, relevant, and valuable to the business. Ask the CFO for assistance in recruiting other senior leaders to a steering committee.

Finally, in a worse-case scenario, leverage passionately supportive leaders wherever you can find them. To do this, approach a respected leader with whom you have worked on providing valuable learning solutions or who really needs your learning services. Request his or her personal mentorship to guide the learning function, and enlist him or her to help you add more members to your governance committee.

The bottom line: Do not go it alone—engage leaders in some level of governance assistance!

Creating and Using a Charter for Your Governance Body

When you are ready to start recruiting governance group members, you will need an initial charter describing the group's purpose and its members' roles. Once your governance group convenes, there will be opportunities to further refine and align your activities in keeping with your charter, building a further sense of ownership among your members.

Charters provide clarity and manage expectations. Without an agreed-upon charter, the governance group is like a boat without a rudder, and it will not take long for your business leaders to become frustrated with the lack of clarity and view their participation as having little value. To prevent this, consider how to design a charter that clearly defines the group's responsibilities and members' specific duties. But this charter does not have to be cumbersome—it can be as simple as the one depicted in figure 4-4.

Figure 4-4. Ingersoll Rand University Charter

Strategy Board Charter

Purpose:

The Corporate University Strategy Board will be a coalition of senior leaders responsible for overseeing the strategy associated with sustaining and maintaining the corporate university. The charter for the strategy board is to set policy direction for and review the operation of the corporate university.

The Strategy Board will be responsible for

- Maintaining the corporate university alignment with the mission and direction of the company.
- Defining policy as it relates to the corporate university in areas such as funding, quality standards, measurements, etc.
- Discussing and resolving issues encompassing the *overall* corporate university curriculum after reviewing evaluation feedback.
- Communicating the company's commitment to the development of employees and the success of the corporate university.
- Involving leaders in sponsorship and teaching.
- Reviewing the outcomes of the investment in learning.

Membership:

- The Corporate University Strategy Board will consist of senior leaders, who have diverse roles and business backgrounds that represent the interests of the enterprise. Some of these positions will be rotating with board members serving 18-month terms. These assignments will be staggered in order to provide continuity.

Strategy Board members should

- Have a broad prospective on the future needs of the organization.
- Be an ambassador for the corporate university by interpreting, communicating, and marketing the organization's mission.
- Be willing to actively participate and attend meetings as required.

Source: Ingersoll Rand University, 2010

Planning Your Governance Group's Meetings

The first priority in planning your governance group's meetings is to seek out a key senior leader to serve as the sponsor for your governance group. Ideally, for governance at the level of a strategy board, this sponsor should be your CEO. Most governance groups at this level meet three or four times a year. Work with your sponsor to craft meeting agendas.

If your CEO's busy schedule prohibits him or her from giving hands-on agenda support, seek out another senior leader from within your strategy board who has the respect and ear of the CEO. For regional, curriculum, and enterprise learning councils, enlist one of the most senior leaders as your council sponsor. Ensure that the leaders from whom you seek advice are seen as credible, strong performers in your business.

Meetings can vary in length and content based on the level of governance. For most of your governance meetings, two to four hours in length is optimal. To minimize potential travel and time away from the office, try to tie the scheduling of your governance meetings to other scheduled meetings of senior leaders. Business leaders appreciate the convenience, and perhaps one less airport security line. Large organizations typically have an annual calendar. If this is the case, schedule and communicate your meeting dates well in advance.

For strategy board governance agendas, you may want use an annual theme for your discussions, such as social networking technology for learning. This creates continuity and gives a cadence to the meetings. To create additional continuity, you may also want to use standard agenda items, such as time set aside for the "voice of the customer," when you obtain input from the members of your governing committee about customers' preferences regarding your learning solutions and processes. Because these committee members travel and interact with many employees across the company, they are a good source of this customer information.

In communicating the agenda for each governance group meeting, specify and communicate your desired meeting outcomes to your group members. For each agenda item, are you seeking directional approval, seeking a final decision, simply informing, or seeking input? This helps frame your expectations vis-à-vis the leaders and provides more organization to your meetings. And ensure that your strategy board agenda items are truly strategic. Of course, your strategic agenda items should be relevant and aligned to the company's strategic issues. Figure 4-5 gives an example of an actual Strategy Board Agenda.

Use external thought leaders to both educate and drive your strategic agenda for learning. Expert, outside thinking helps open new paradigms

Figure 4-5. Agenda for a Strategy Board Meeting

- Welcome New Members
  - xxxx – Operational Excellence College Sponsor
  - xxxx – Sales/Marketing College Sponsor
  - xxxx – CIO
- Discussion Topics
  1. Enterprise Learning Structure
     - Decision needed: Approval on corporate university strategic direction and scope
  2. Corporate University Governance Model
     - Decision needed: Approval of revised model
  3. Sector Funding Model Review
     - Decision needed: Approval on model
  4. Impact Evaluation Overview
     - Inform only
  5. Corporate University Learning Technology Strategy
     - Information/Demo on Learning Technology by XXXXXX. "The Use of Blended Learning and Communities of Practice in Global Companies"
     - Decision needed to move forward on eLearning Suite for IR

XXXXX is President and CEO of XXXXX, a research and advisory services firm that provides guidance on corporate learning to seniors or executives at companies like UBS, Microsoft, Toyota, Pfizer, M&M Ma,s and many others. XXXX has more than 20 years' experience working in all aspects of creating high-performance organizations through learning and performance, including talent management strategies, leadership development, learning technologies, and measuring performance and business impact.

of thought in your governance meetings. Business leaders are accustomed to monitoring external trends and research to inform their work. Providing your strategy board with related premeeting reading helps set the context for meeting discussions, educates, and engages members before the meeting. Be careful to screen academic experts and reading materials to make sure that their communication style will resonate with business practicality versus theory.

Take adequate time to prepare for your governance meetings. Prepare your meeting content for concise communication and ensure that it reflects the language of business, not the jargon of learning. Use quantitative data when available. In completing these tasks, your governance sponsor can be extremely helpful in guiding you. For strategy board meetings, make certain that your agenda content remains at the strategic versus tactical levels. To increase engagement during the meeting, prepare comments and questions to start discussions.

Postmeeting Follow-Up

Business leaders expect follow-up and action. After each meeting of your governance group, create a summary of key decisions and actions like these:

- The topics covered, such as how to leverage the synergies of the multiple training departments across the company.
- Decisions made to establish a companywide, mandatory learning council for training leaders across the company.
- Particular actions—for example, "By end of year, launch the Company Learning Council."

This summary confirms to your governance leaders' your alignment with their meeting contributions and demonstrates implementation actions. The summary will be useful for those members unable to attend the meeting and also serves as a reference tool for all. Figure 4-6 includes an actual example of a postmeeting summary.

Recognizing the Leaders Serving on Your Governance Board

By serving on a governance board or council, your business leaders are committing their most precious asset: time. Recognizing their contributions should be part of your overall governance system. There are a variety of easily deployed recognition approaches. Here are a few possibilities:

- letter of thanks from the CEO (or another C-suite leader)
- handwritten thank-you notes specifying a particular meeting contribution
- photos of governance group members in a prominent location—a "Hall of Fame"
- wall plaque citing their participation in the governance board/council
- relevant business book with a handwritten bookmark of thanks from you
- engraved desk item.

You will have a better sense of what recognition approach will work best within your organization.

Figure 4-6. Strategy Board Meeting Notes

Topics Covered:

- Strategic direction for the combined IRU-BOS integration into new entity of Enterprise Learning
- Trends in Knowledge Transfer
- Extension of the Learning Management System (LMS) to hourly and other external populations
- Preview of initial 2011 Learning Plan themes

Decisions:

- The Enterprise Learning Management System (LMS) managed by Enterprise Learning is the sole learning management system for Ingersoll Rand
- Expand use of the Enterprise Learning Management System (LMS) to deliver and track training for hourly employees and dealers/distributors and customers

Actions:

- LMS expansion (inclusive of identification of LMS Leaders in the Sectors, enterprise-wide standards and governance, migration of other LMS systems to the Enterprise LMS, addition of E-Commerce capability)
- Drive BOS as a living process (inclusive of links to GTE and Goal Deployment, dissemination to end users and process improvement processes –PDCA)
- Identify initial knowledge transfer projects (e.g., M&A Integration learnings, CEES, Energy Engineers Community of Practice, LaCrosse engineering/R&D)
- Globalize IRMBA and other IRU Curriculum
- Scope and obtain funding for upgrade of Herbert H. Henkel Learning Center
- Leverage existing service tools/ training as we create new Service School

Our next meeting is Wednesday, October 20, 8:00 – 10:00 AM EST. This will be an abbreviated two hour meeting, designed for virtual attendance. The purpose will be to review/approve the 2010 Learning Plan to ensure strategic alignment and prioritization with business strategy.

Thank you for your thought leadership and engagement with Enterprise Learning; it is truly a differentiator for us.

Rita Smith

Designing and Developing Learning Solutions

For the most part, governing bodies set the overall strategic direction for the learning function. The learning solutions you create reflect the execution of this strategic direction. The design and development of learning solutions offers a tremendous opportunity to engage business leaders and stakeholders. This engagement strategy presents this design and development effort as a learning process in which business leaders can be heavily involved—or even lead. It incorporates a collaborative, rapid design model, which ensures that the solution is business relevant, is aligned with business priorities, and is truly "owned" by the business. Thus, it is helpful to view the design and development of learning as a new product development (NPD) process. Using the framework of an existing business process, such as NPD, builds credibility for the learning function. Once again, the language and tools of business are highly applicable to the learning function.

Setting the Context: The New Product Development Process

In the language of business, your design and development of learning solutions can be viewed as an NPD process. You will find that "NPD" is a frequently used business acronym, and it is probable that your business is currently using an NPD process. (Your marketing business leaders can direct you to the specific model used by your particular organization.) Designing and developing learning solutions entails a series of related activities that lead to the delivery of a learning solution. In viewing your design and development as an NPD process, you gain credibility with your business leaders because they are familiar with this process, and your use of it thus indicates that you are following systematic business rigor. Enlisting business leaders to help design and develop your learning solutions also gives these products a high level of business relevance.

This engagement strategy also minimizes, if not eliminates, the endless "prove your value" conversations that those involved in learning functions typically experience. By being willing to participate in learning governance and sponsorship, your business leaders showed that they had decided the learning solution was important. Now these leaders are designing and developing the learning solutions, thus ensuring their business relevance and impact. They help you with business-specific learning objectives and application exercises. Finally, your leaders have come to have strong ownership of the learning solution and thus have become strong "ambassadors" for both the learning solution and your learning function.

The most common, collaborative NPD process is based on the model presented in Robert G. Cooper's book *Winning at New Products Accelerating: The Process from Idea to Launch* (1986). Cooper refers to this process as "Stage Gate." It is divided into five stages that constitute key activities and deliverables (there is also a pre-NPD discovery stage, which is akin to an initial idea generation and a high-level needs assessment):

- Stage 1, *Scoping*, includes research and deeper investigation of the need. In learning terms, this is where you obtain a sponsor for the potential learning solution.

- Stage 2, *Building the Business Case*, includes product and project definition, project justification, and a project plan. This is typically where funding for the new product is approved. In learning terms, this is where you have obtained approval and funding for a new learning solution.
- Stage 3, *Development*, is the actual detailed design and development of the new product or learning solution. (This stage is the focus of this section).
- Stage 4, *Testing and Validation*, incorporates trials in the marketplace, or what learning professionals refer to as pilot programs.
- Stage 5, *Launch*, is full production, marketing, and selling. In the language of learning, this equates to the ongoing delivery of programs.

Each stage is followed by a quality control decision gate. Multifunctional teams—such as marketing, customers, suppliers, engineering, and operations—work together through the stages and gates. All key stakeholders are engaged, resulting in speedy product development. At each gate, a multifunctional leadership group conducts a review against pre-established criteria. Review decisions can range from stopping to continuing to improving the new product's design and development. Investments increase as you move through the NPD process, ensuring that the investment risk is managed.

The discipline of the Stage Gate approach also ensures a strong market orientation, with customer feedback built into the process. Other benefits include higher product quality, minimal reworking, and the most efficient and effective use of resources.

This inclusive NPD framework is becoming more and more important because its participatory ethos fits so well with the way that companies are increasing the internal and external collaboration they use in their NPD efforts. They are including more and more customers and suppliers in real-time collaboration. This trend toward increasingly collaborative design is a result of both intense global market pressures and improvements in communication technologies.

The NPD process is easily transferable to your learning solutions. By collaborating with your business leaders, together you create learning solutions that in turn

- lead to higher levels of alignment and buy-in
- give your learning a strong business relevance
- validate the need to make the required investment in the learning solution.

Therefore, every strategic learning solution should have an executive business sponsor. And as you and your business sponsor come to agree on success metrics and jointly request the necessary funding, this process in a very visible way displays your alignment with the business, which diminishes the pressure to "prove the value of learning."

More and more, companies are viewing their vendors or suppliers as partners with a stake in their products' successful life cycles. One key way to form these partnerships is to engage your potential suppliers in the design process. Thus, these suppliers benefit from hearing about the business needs firsthand from the business's leaders. They also get a sense of the context for various requirements such as delivery mode and cost management. Extending these same principles of engaging your learning vendors and/or suppliers in helping to design your learning solutions means that these external partners will gain a whole new level of partnership with you—including a much deeper understanding of the context of the business issue and the business-defined learning requirements.

As you engage these business leaders, you will find that most of them do not want to become involved in levels of evaluation and conversations about return on investment. Instead, they are more interested in a rigorous, systematic business process that creates a value-adding learning solution. Think of the information systems or marketing functions within your organizations. They have stepped off the constant "prove your worth" merry-go-round. Like these functions, if your learning solution is driven by strategic need, created to fulfill business requirements, and delivered in a way that works with the realities of business, positive results should logically follow. Thus, by engaging the business leaders in the actual design and development of learning solutions, they come to co-own these solutions.

Introducing the Rapid Design Team Meeting

As you have seen, stage 3 of the NPD process includes *design* and *development*. In learning language, these are the "D and D" of the familiar instructional design model ADDIE—analysis, design, development, implementation, and evaluation. Rather than replacing instructional design models such as ADDIE, the NPD process complements them by adding more business rigor and thus strategic alignment.

The Rapid Design Team meeting is a best practice strategy for eliciting leader engagement that you can use in designing and developing learning solutions. This type of meeting entails a collaborative, rapid design session focused on the capabilities of training to achieve business results. The initial discussion focuses on the desired business results and performance indicators and the critical behaviors required to achieve the targeted results. From this, key skills, knowledge, and attitudes capabilities are identified. These translate into potential learning objectives. What makes the Rapid Design Team meeting particularly effective is the role business leaders play in identifying

- business results
- critical behaviors
- necessary capabilities.

The learning function participates to contribute adult learning expertise, but clearly this is a business-driven design session. Meetings typically include two days of engaging business leaders, development suppliers (if applicable), target audience members, and learning professionals in the design and development of a learning solution. The key outcomes from the meeting are

- a learning solution design
- development supplier selection (if applicable)
- a development project plan.

If you do not use outsourced suppliers to develop your learning solutions, you can adapt the Rapid Design Team meeting format to your internal model by omitting the supplier participation and replacing it with an internally created design. The overall meeting will still yield a business-designed and -developed learning solution. Notes on adapting the meeting to your internal development model are given in each step and in each tool.

A successful Rapid Design Team comprises key business leaders, content experts, and target audience members. To ensure a highly business relevant design, diversity factors such as geographic and/or business unit representation are key. Participating on a Rapid Design Team is an ideal developmental opportunity for high potential talent. They are exposed to senior business leaders from across the company and thus are able to contribute to a significant, strategic learning solution. Although your business leaders may be familiar with collaborative design sessions through their own NPD process, most likely the Rapid Design Team is a new concept for them to associate with the learning function. You will thus need to clearly communicate its purpose and their roles and responsibilities.

The main framework of Rapid Design Team meetings is the High Impact Learning Map (HILM) developed by Robert Brinkerhoff. An HILM is a visual representation of how learning is linked to business impact. It begins with business goals and results and then moves to the performance or critical behaviors needed to achieve the business goals and results. From the performance and critical behaviors indicators, capability requirements are identified. The key skills, knowledge, and attitudes needed to ultimately achieve the business goals and results are transformed into learning objectives. Discussion of potential learning solutions is purposely designed last and is derived from business goals and results. A detailed illustration of an HILM appears later in chapter 4 (see figures 4-15 and 4-16 later in the chapter).

For externally developed learning, there is additional uniqueness in that the Rapid Design Team meeting engages potential learning development suppliers in the actual meeting. Finalist suppliers are invited to attend and then create a real-time proposal for a potential learning solution. The team members vote and select the "best" supplier. Again, the business leaders are intimately engaged in shaping the learning solution. Key success metrics for the meeting process include

- feedback from the Rapid Design Team in assessing the value, efficiency, and effectiveness of the meeting
- learning solution quality, as evaluated by learners as highly relevant to the business
- repeat participation of Rapid Design Team members in future team meetings.

The rest of this subsection provides a step-by-step road map for implementing a Rapid Design Team meeting in your company. To give an overview, figure 4-7 provides a process map of a meeting where external vendors are included. And figure 4-8 depicts a meeting where the learning solution is developed internally.

Creating a Team Charter

Although your business leaders may be quite familiar with an NPD design and development process, associating this with the learning function may be new for them. Therefore, it is essential that you draft a team charter that clearly articulates the purpose, roles, responsibilities, and outcomes for the Rapid Design Team meeting. The scope of what is required of these roles should be clear to ensure that team members are fully aware of their commitment. The charter should also include a detailed profile of each team member. Two sample charters are shown in figures 4-9 and 4-10, representing both the externally developed learning and internally developed learning models.

The Team's Membership

In chapter 3, we saw that it is critical to have a business sponsor for *all* your strategic learning solutions. You will find that your business sponsor is a key resource to coach you on appropriate team membership. Your business sponsor has line-of-sight to help you identify key leaders, subject matter experts, and potential target audience members. In addition,

Figure 4-7. Map of a Rapid Design Team Meeting with External Vendors

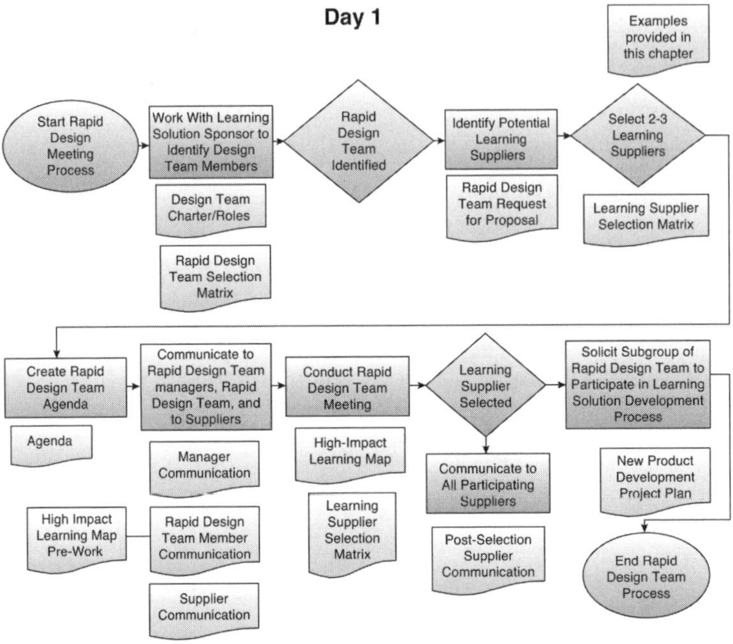

Day 1

Examples provided in this chapter

Start Rapid Design Meeting Process

Work With Learning Solution Sponsor to Identify Design Team Members

Design Team Charter/Roles

Rapid Design Team Selection Matrix

Rapid Design Team Identified

Identify Potential Learning Suppliers

Rapid Design Team Request for Proposal

Select 2-3 Learning Suppliers

Learning Supplier Selection Matrix

Create Rapid Design Team Agenda

Agenda

High Impact Learning Map Pre-Work

Communicate to Rapid Design Team managers, Rapid Design Team, and to Suppliers

Manager Communication

Rapid Design Team Member Communication

Supplier Communication

Conduct Rapid Design Team Meeting

High-Impact Learning Map

Learning Supplier Selection Matrix

Learning Supplier Selected

Communicate to All Participating Suppliers

Post-Selection Supplier Communication

Solicit Subgroup of Rapid Design Team to Participate in Learning Solution Development Process

New Product Development Project Plan

End Rapid Design Team Process

Please note validated learning opportunity and program sponsorship is input to the Rapid Design Meeting Process. This input process is discussed in the Business Learning Needs Process found in chapter 3. Upon completion of the Rapid Design Meeting Process, the New Product Development Process begins.

the talent management processes within your business can identify high potential employees who could benefit from the development opportunity of participating on a global design team. Make certain that your sponsor has final approval of your Rapid Design Team's membership. A planning matrix such as the one shown in figure 4-11 will help you design your team's composition.

For multinational companies, it is critically important to create global diversity on your Rapid Design Team. Regardless if your company is global, a diverse team will yield a better learning solution. In figure 4-11, the sample team selection matrix, moving from left to right across the matrix, important membership criteria in this example include representation from all business units and the corporate center. In addition, all global regions are represented to ensure global applicability of the learning solution. The learning group representation includes curriculum, deployment, and instructional technology representation. A representative from sourcing is included. Varying levels of the target audience are also included. Use this tool to perform a final assessment of your Rapid Design Team's composition. In addition, you may want to use a tool like this to create a searchable database of business leaders engaged in your overall design and development efforts.

Figure 4-8 Map of a Rapid Design Team Meeting with an Internal Learning Solution

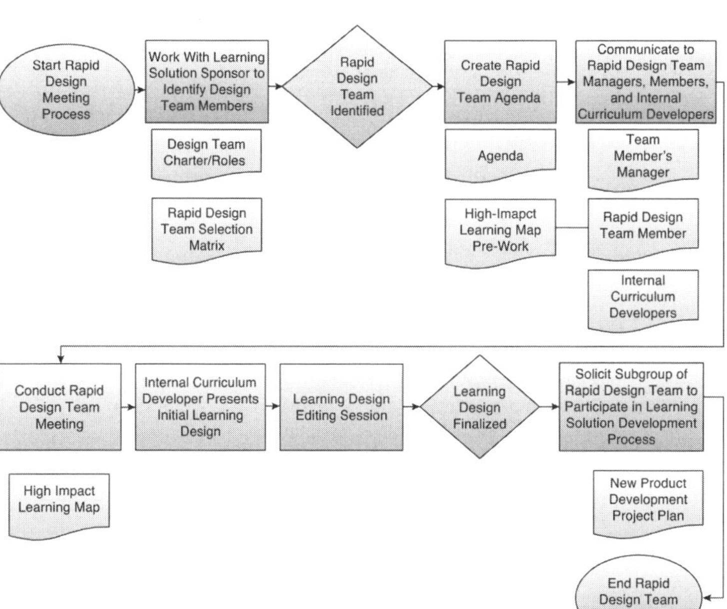

Please note validated learning opportunity and program sponsorship is input to the Rapid Design Meeting Process. This input process is discussed in the Business Learning Needs Process found in chapter 3. Upon completion of the Rapid Design Meeting Process, the New Product Development Process begins.

Figure 4-9. Rapid Design Team Charter for Externally Developed Learning

Team Purpose	To ensure Company programs provide business-relevant, market-driven learning solutions that meet enterprise-wide education needs and are based upon Company leadership, general management, and functional competencies. The team will be involved in all of the following design and development stages: • Creating the business requirements • Analyzing needs assessment information • Designing • Supporting the pilot program
Team Structure	Teams consist of • Program sponsor – business leader • Cross-functional, cross-geography, multi-level business leaders • Company sourcing representative • Learning function professionals – learning program manager • Design and development suppliers
Sponsor's Role	The Sponsor's major responsibilities include • Serve as an advocate to help promote the program • Assist in identifying global business representatives to serve as subject matter experts (SMEs) on the design and development • Send letter or other communications drafted by learning function to various audiences – Needs assessment audience – Program • Help drive program input on design and development • Be actively engaged in the program pilot (i.e., kick off program, etc.) • Potentially teach a segment of the program • Conduct pre-work conference call with participants to set context for the learning
Learning Program Manager's Role	The Program Manager's major responsibilities include • Share research and best practices and assessment data • Develop project plan • Organize team meetings, create agendas, and document action items • Drive team to complete action items and deliverables • Escalate issues or concerns as required • Communicates team plans, changes, and the impacts to the organization

Rapid Design Team – Roles and Responsibilities

Major responsibilities include
- Review and analyze assessment data
- Provide direction on solution(s) design
- Review and give feedback on resources, processes, and tools that are developed
- Participant in piloting of solutions
- Evaluate pilot results
- Ensure revisions based on pilot results are completed (if needed)
- Hand off project to Implementation and Maintenance Teams
- Serve as an advocate to help promote the development of solutions throughout IR
- Participate actively in team meetings
- Complete action items or requests on time
- Represent accurately your area, but make decisions based on the interest of the enterprise company vs. any individual function
- Communicate with other team members as needed to exchange information, share concerns, and provide feedback
- Champion the team's decisions with all areas of the business
- Identify and share issues/concerns within the team first, so the team can decide what needs to be escalated to sponsor or senior leadership

Rapid Design Team Membership Profile

Rapid Design teams will consist of 8–10 business leaders. The combined team should have representation from the sectors, functions, and global regions as well as various levels of experience and years of service.

Characteristics of the ideal team member include
- Displays a passion for continual learning and the development of IR leaders
- Has an enterprise-wide mindset
- Thinks globally
- Has some knowledge of the program content being developed.
- Willingness to actively participate and attend meetings as required

Frequency of Meetings

- An initial 2-day meeting will be conducted to design the program, select the supplier, and review development project plan. (Virtual attendees will be accommodated, but in-person attendance is preferred.)
- The team will meet virtually once a week (maximum 1 hour) to start, moving to every other week as timeline permits or a duration of 3-4 months depending on the complexity of the program.
- Agendas will be developed and communicated prior to each meeting.

Identifying Potential Learning Suppliers

If you use outside resources to develop your learning solutions, the step of identifying potential learning suppliers is ready for your implementation. However, if your learning solutions are developed internally, you will substitute your learning development staff for external learning development suppliers in the Rapid Design Team meeting. For internal development models, you will omit the steps of searching for and selecting potential external supplier finalists, given that your development is completed internally.

For externally developed learning, your initial supplier research will enable you to create a request for proposals for potential suppliers. The Rapid Design Team meeting RFP highlights the specific steps of your suppler selection process: It includes a description of the scope of the work you are requesting, and it also specifies your selection criteria and processes. Figure 4-12 provides a representative excerpt for such an RFP describing the Rapid Design Team supplier selection process.

Selecting Your Supplier Finalists

There is probably a host of learning suppliers from which to choose. Before the Rapid Design Team meeting, it is the responsibility of those supervising the learning function to screen responses and select a workable number of appropriate suppliers. The suppliers who are selected to participate in your team meeting and interact with your business leaders should be prescreened to ensure that they are viable potential partners. Your selection criteria for suppliers may vary according to what is important to your company:

- One criterion could be the supplier's global expertise. Look for evidence that the supplier has a global network to deliver its services and has documented experience in a number of global geographies. Ask questions on how it localizes and translates its learning materials. Inquire on how it manages quality around the globe.
- Another criterion could be the supplier's ability to transfer its capability for internal delivery within your company.

Figure 4-10. Rapid Design Team Charter for Internally Developed Learning

Team Purpose	To ensure Company programs provide business-relevant, market-driven learning solutions that meet enterprise-wide education needs and are based upon Company leadership, general management, and functional competencies. The team will be involved in all of the following design and development stages: • Creating the business requirements • Analyzing needs assessment information • Designing • Supporting the pilot program
Team Structure	Teams consist of • Program sponsor – business leader • Cross-functional, cross-geography, multi-level business leaders • Company sourcing representative • Learning function professionals-learning program manager • Design and development suppliers

Sponsor's Role	The Sponsor's major responsibilities include
	• Serve as an advocate to help promote the program
	• Assist in identifying global business representatives to serve as subject matter experts (SMEs) on the design and development
	• Send letter or other communications drafted by learning function to various audiences
	  – Needs assessment audience
	  – Program participants
	• Help drive program input on design and development
	• Be actively engaged in the program pilot (i.e., kick off program, etc.)
	• Potentially teach a segment of the program
	• Conduct pre-work conference call with participants to set context for the learning

Learning Program Manager's Role	The Program Manager's major responsibilities include • Share research and best practices and assessment data • Develop project plan • Organize team meetings, create agendas, and document action items • Drive team to complete action items and deliverables • Escalate issues or concerns as required • Communicates team plans, changes, and the impacts to the organization

Rapid Design Team – Roles and Responsibilities	Major responsibilities include • Review and analyze assessment data • Provide direction on solution(s) design • Review and give feedback on resources, processes, and tools that are developed • Participant in piloting of solutions • Evaluate pilot results • Ensure revisions based on pilot results are completed (if needed) • Hand off project to Implementation and Maintenance Teams • Serve as an advocate to help promote the development of solutions throughout IR • Participate actively in team meetings • Complete action items or requests on time • Represent accurately your area, but make decisions based on the interest of the enterprise company, vs. any individual function • Communicate with other team members as needed to exchange information, share concerns, and provide feedback • Champion the team's decisions with all areas of the business • Identify and share issues/concerns within the team first, so the team can decide what needs to be escalated to sponsor or senior leadership
Rapid Design Team Membership Profile	Rapid Design teams will consist of 8 – 10 business leaders. The combined team should have representation from the sectors, functions, and global regions as well as various levels of experience and years of service. Characteristics of the ideal team member include • Displays a passion for continual learning and the development of IR leaders • Has a enterprise-wide mindset • Thinks globally • Has some knowledge of the program content being developed. • Willingness to actively participate and attend meetings as required
Frequency of Meetings	• An initial 2-day meeting will be conducted to design the program, select the supplier, and review development project plan. (Virtual attendees will be accommodated, but in-person attendance is preferred.) • The team will meet virtually once a week (maximum 1 hour) to start, moving to every other week as timeline permits or a duration of 3-4 months depending on the complexity of the program • Agendas will be developed and communicated prior to each meeting
Internal Learning Developer	• Assist in learning curriculum research • Participate as a Rapid Design Team Member • Create an initial learning design as an output of Day 1 of the Rapid Design Team Meeting • Incorporate edits into the finalized learning design • Serve as lead learning developer for this project

Examine its learning materials to ensure that they are designed for internal trainers' use. Explore the supplier's process for training the trainer.

- A final criterion could be the supplier's ability to drive down costs. Ask for examples of how it has lowered costs for other clients. An example could be how it has provided an e-learning segment to replace a face-to-face training day.

Before staff members completed the tool given in figure 4-13, six suppliers were originally screened as potential partners. An initial assessment of the suppliers' capabilities left three potential suppliers remaining. These three suppliers are evaluated at a deeper level using the selection criteria described below. Typically, the field is narrowed to two or three supplier finalists.

Planning the Agenda for Your Team Meeting

For externally developed learning, the agenda for your Rapid Design Team meeting has four key components:

- a current state analysis
- a high impact learning map exercise
- supplier presentations
- the final selection of a supplier partner.

A full two days are used for this meeting.

However, for internally developed learning solutions, the agenda for your Rapid Design Team meeting will include

- a current state analysis
- a high impact learning map
- a review of the initial internally developed design.

Note that this meeting runs the equivalent of one full day. The agenda reflects a half-day session on day 1 and the remaining half-day session on day 2. Your internal learning developers will require the time overnight to create an initial learning design for review on day 2.

Figure 4-11. A Planning Matrix for Selecting the Members of Your Rapid Design Team

Rapid Design Team Meeting Selection Matrix for (Insert Program Name Here)

(Use this template to ensure you have representatives on your design team from each of the areas listed below)

#	Design Team Member Name	Title	Business Unit Name						Region				Enterprise Learning					Company Sourcing Rep	Target Audience	Level			Location (City/State/Country)	Phone Numbers	Manager
									North America	Latin America	Europe/Middle East	Asia	Technology	Deployment	Curriculums					Individual	People Manager	Senior Manager*			
1	(Sponsor)																								
2	(Curriculum Lead)																								
3																									
4																									
5																									
6																									
7																									
8																									
9																									
10																									
11																									
12																									
13																									
14																									
15																									

In addition, having a team dinner further engages the Rapid Design Team's members with each other and your learning function. A one- or two-day meeting is a substantial time commitment for business leaders, who will thus expect a meeting that offers a level of value equivalent with the valuable time they have invested. Therefore, careful planning and effective execution are critical. For examples of both externally and internally developed versions of a two-day meeting agenda, see figure 4-14.

Communicating the Team Meeting's Results to Key Stakeholders

You need to communicate the Rapid Design Team's process, logistics, roles and responsibilities, and premeeting preparation to these stakeholders:

- The managers of the potential team meeting invitees. (You are seeking approval for those who report directly to them to

Figure 4-12. Excerpt from a Request for Proposal for a Rapid Design Team's Supplier Selection Process

Scope of Work

The purpose of this request is to identify Strategic Partners who will work with our company curriculum managers and design teams to design, develop, and/or deliver programs in accordance with our learning function's NPD Phase Gate process illustrated later in this document.

The supplier selection process for design, development, and delivery of each program is as follows:

1. Suppliers complete this request for proposal with standard pricing for design, development, and delivery.
2. We will choose a select group of strategic partners based on methodology, experience, subject matter expertise, and standard pricing, and set up master contract agreements with these suppliers.
3. In the project scoping phase of each program, we identify one or more of the previously selected strategic partners to attend a two-to-three day program design meeting. During the first day of the meeting, our curriculum manager and design team will create a High Impact Learning Map that identifies the learning specifications for the program. During the second day of this meeting, each of the strategic partners will be expected to present their proposal for achieving the learning needs identified in day one of the meeting.
4. Following the presentations, the supplier will be selected to develop the program. The selection will be based on the design concept, methodology, experience, subject matter expertise, and standard pricing.

Source: Ingersoll Rand University, 2010.

Figure 4-13. Rapid Design Team Sample Selection Criteria (Ratings Partially Completed for Example Purposes)

Rapid Design Tema Supplier Selection Criteria

Rating Key: High Medium Low

Criteria	Supplier 1	Supplier 2	Supplier 3	Comments
Expertise and Thought Leadership Is the supplier recognized nationally/internationally as leader on this topic?	H	H	M	Supplier 3 is stronger nationally vs. internationally
Partnership Does the supplier demonstrate desire to partner with us?	H	H	H	
Reputation Is the supplier easy to work with? Are they known for getting projects completed as scheduled? What is the quality of their deliverables?	H	H	L	Reference checks and benchmarking contacts indicate Supplier 3 isn't consistent in meeting project deadlines.
Distinguished Faculty (in this domain) Does proposed faculty have the necessary expertise? Are they recognized nationally/internationally?	H	H	L	Supplier 3 has only nationally recognized faculty.
Integration with Our Company To what extent is the supplier's approach to learning consistent with our company's learning philosophy? Are the concept models used by the supplier consistent with our other learning programs? Does the supplier utilize a variety of teaching methodologies to enhance learning?	H	M	M	Supplier 2 insists on using their proprietary models which aren't consistent with models in our other learning programs. Supplier 3 hasn't worked with a leaders as teachers model.
Global Resources does the supplier have faculty/designers/developers representative of non-US cultures?				

Criteria	Supplier 1	Supplier 2	Supplier 3	Comments
Does the supplier have resources outside of their company that they can tap into?				
Global expertise Has the supplier developed previous programs that were deployed globally?				
Build internal capacity Does the supplier desire to transfer knowledge in such a way that it reduces costs and increases IRU capacity to deliver?				
Involve our executives Has the supplier developed learning solutions where business leaders were involved in the design of the program?				
Flexibility Is the supplier willing and able to adapt to meet our needs?				
Cost Are the supplier's costs competitive and in alignment with our budget?				
Drive down costs Does the supplier look for ways to reduce costs where possible?				

Source: Ingersoll Rand University, 2010.

participate in the meeting. This communication must precede a direct invitation to the meeting team member.)

- Business leaders invited to serve as team members.
- Supplier finalists selected for participation in the team meeting *or* your internal learning developers
- The business sponsor of the learning solution.

In addition to information regarding the meeting, the business Rapid Design Team members will also receive instructions for completion of prework, which asks the business leaders to begin mapping the linkages of potential learning and job performance to the desired business goals and results. The prework tool is Brinkerhoff's High Impact Learning Map.

Using the High Impact Learning Map as the Framework for Your Team Meeting

The High Impact Learning Map (HILM), mentioned earlier in this chapter, is the primary framework for your Rapid Design Team meeting. It is a visual representation of how learning is linked to business impact. HILMs are used to

- analyze the business impact that is needed from learning
- identify learning and performance requirements
- clarify expectations for learning results
- guide measurement and evaluation.

Robert Brinkerhoff developed the initial concept of the High Impact Learning Map. His seminal books on this topic include *High Impact Learning* (Brinkerhoff and Apking 2001) and the *Success Case Method* (Brinkerhoff 2003). Both books are invaluable to gaining a greater understanding of how to align learning with business results. Because the HILM is the framework for your Rapid Design Team meeting, this subsection provides you with a basic overview of HILMs. Figure 4-15 illustrates a partially completed example of an HILM template for a sales profitability learning solution.

Figure 4-14. Sample Two-Day Rapid Design Team Meeting Agendas

Rapid Design Team Sample Agenda—Externally Developed Learning

Agenda: <Insert Program or Learning Solution Name> Rapid Design Team Meeting

Meeting Objectives The goals of the meeting are to

- Identify the desired business outcomes of the program
- Determine what existing materials may be used as source documents
- Agree on supplier selection for program development

Meeting logistics Date: <Insert date(s)>
Time: <Insert time for each day>
Place: <Insert location and icon>

Pre-work Review materials and captures your preliminary thoughts for the attached High Impact Learning Map (HILM) document. We will spend a good deal of time working on this during the two day session.
Identify thing, and be prepared to share any existing, relevant materials that could be utilized is the development of this program. If you would like for us to make copies of any materials please provide soft copies of this documentation to RJ prior to the meeting. "include contact name"

Agenda Day 1

Time	Topic	Who
8:00-8:45	Welcome, Agenda, Introductions, and Sponsor Comments	Curriculum Lead Sponsor
8:45-9:00	Program Development Process and Design Team Roles	Curriculum Lead
9:00-9:45	Current State	ALL
9:45-10:00	BREAK	ALL
12:00-12:45	High Impact Learning Map Exercise	ALL
10:00-12:00	LUNCH	ALL
12:45-1:15	Existing Materials Review	ALL
1:15-2:00	Design Team Meeting with 1st Supplier (Supplier(s) gets opportunity to ask any clarifying question they may have around Content Objectives, Process, etc)	ALL 1st Supplier
2:00-2:15	BREAK	ALL
2:15-3:00	Design Team Meeting with 2nd Supplier	ALL 2nd Supplier
3:00-3:45	Design Team Meeting with 3rd Supplier	ALL 3rd Supplier
3:45-4:00	BREAK	ALL
4:00-4:45	Revert HLM and Self Expectations for Suppliers	ALL
4:45-5:00	First Day Wrap up	Curriculum Lead
5:30-6:30	Team Dinner	ALL

Agenda: <Insert Program or Learning Solution Name> Rapid Design Team Meeting, *Continued*

Agenda Day 2

Time	Topic	Who
8:00-8:30	Supplier Scoring Criteria	Curriculum Lead
8:30-9:45	1st Supplier Presentation	1st Supplier
9:45-10:00	BREAK	ALL
10:00-11:15	Debrief and Score Presentation	ALL
11:15-12:30	2nd Supplier Presentation	2nd Supplier
12:30-1:15	LUNCH	ALL
1:15-1:45	Debrief and Score Presentation	ALL
1:45-3:00	3rd Supplier Presentation	3rd Supplier
3:00-3:15	BREAK	ALL
3:15-3:45	Debrief and Score Presentation	ALL
3:45-5:00	Select supplier and/or identify Fellow up actions needed–Discuss Next Steps	ALL

Source: Ingersoll Rand University, 2010

Rapid Design Team Sample Agenda-Internally Developed Learning

Agenda Meeting: <Insert Program or Learning Solution Name> Rapid Design Team

Meeting Objectives

The goals of the meeting are to

- Identify the desired business outcomes of the program
- Determine what existing materials may be used as source documents
- Agree on vendor selection for program development

Meeting Logistics

Date: < Insert date(s) >
Time: < Insert time for each day>
Place: < Insert location and room>

Pre-work

Review materials and capture your preliminary thought for the attached High Impact Learning Map (HILM) document. We will spend a good deal of time working on this during the two day session.

Identify, bring, and be prepared to share any existing, relevant materials that could be utilized in the development of the program. If you would like for us to make copies of any materials, please provide softcopies of this documentation to company prior to the meeting. <Include contact name>

Agenda Day 1

Time	Topic	Who
12:30 - 12:45 pm	Welcome, Agenda, Introductions and Sponsor Comments	Curriculum Lead Sponsor
12:45 - 1 pm	Program Development Process and Design Team Role	Curriculum Lead
1:00 - 1:45 pm	Current State	ALL
1:45 - 2:00 pm	BREAK	ALL
2:00 - 4:30 pm	High Impact Learning Map Exercise	ALL
4:30 - 5:00 pm	First Day Wrap-Up/Review Tomorrow's Agenda	Curriculum Lead
6:00 pm	Team Dinner	ALL

Agenda Day 2

Time	Topic	Who
8:00 - 8:30 am	Revisit yesterday's HILM & Introduce today's agenda	Curriculum Lead
8:30 - 9:30 am	Initial Learning Design Presentation	Internal learning developer
9:30 - 9:45 am	BREAK	ALL
9:45 - 10:15 am	Individual edit brainstorming exerciss	ALL
10:15 - 10:45 am	Recap Individual brainstorming edits and create attn by themes	Curriculum Lead/All
10:45 - 11:45 am	Discuss final edits (may be done thru multi-dota voting & discussion)	Curriculum Lead/All
11:45 - 12:00 pm	Wrap up and discuss next steps and roles in the development stage	Curriculum Lead

Source: Ingersoll Rand University, 2010

The HILM has three key components: results, performance, and capability. Subcategories consist of business goals; key results; critical behaviors; and key skills, knowledge, and attitudes. Each subcategory is ultimately asking a key design question of business leaders, for example:

- How will this learning help the business?
- How will the success of the learning be measured?
- How should this learning be applied?
- What performance capabilities will the learning address?

As these questions are answered, they are entered into the HILM template. A category code, such as "BG" for business goals, is used for each entry to make subsequent design discussions easier. The actual design document typically attaches category codes to components of the design, ensuring visible alignment with the HILM. Typically, there are a small number of business goals, and eventually this leads to a robust list of the key skills, knowledge, and attitudes necessary to achieve the business goals.

When creating an HILM like the one given in figure 4-15, begin at the right with business goals and work your way left to specific learning (knowledge, skills, and attitudes) required to achieve the business goals. The HILM focuses on learning requirements for a key job role, such as sales managers. The entire learning solution originates from the business goals. This is followed by the business results that will be necessary to achieve the goals. Critical on-the-job behaviors required to achieve the business results follow. The HILM culminates in a listing of the knowledge, skills, and attitudes that will be necessary to successfully perform the critical job behaviors linked to achieving the desired business goals.

In advance of your meeting, you want the leaders on your Rapid Design Team to be thinking about the critical behaviors, skills, knowledge, and attitudes needed to achieve the predetermined business result. To accomplish this, business leaders are asked to complete an HILM as prework. Include directions on how to use the HILM. Ask your business leaders to identify five to six business goals and key results related

Figure 4-15. A Partially Completed Example of a High Impact Learning Map Template

	Capability	Performance	Results	
Target Audience Job Role	**Key Skills, Knowledge, and Attitudes**	**Critical Behaviors**	**Key Results**	**Business Goals**
Who is target learner?	Learning objectives.... *What performance capabilities will the learning address?*	Important on-the-job behaviors.... *How should this learning be applied?*	Key job results to achieve business objectives..... *How will success of the learning be measured?*	Work unit goals to achieve overall company goals.... *How will this learning help the business?*
PARTIAL EXAMPLE: *Sales Managers*	*(KSA) 1–Understand profitability versus just sales* *(KSA) 2–Create and use a scatterplot analysis to segment customers* *(KSA) 3–Create and analyze waterfall charts*	*(CB) 1–Customer cost/value segmentation for each application* *(CB) 2–Price and profitability dashboards are used to inform investment decisions* *(CB) 3–Product waterfall analysis in use*	*(KR) 1–Invoice to Pocket Price improvement of at least 1%* *(KR) 2–Higher profitability margin per sales employee*	*(BG)1–Increase pricing profit margins*

Source: Adapted from *High Impact Learning: Strategies for Leveraging Business Results from Training*, by Robert O. Brinkerhoff and Anne M. Apking (Cambridge, MA: Perseus, 2001). Used by permission.

to the overall topic of the team meeting. They should be instructed to include 5 to 10 critical behaviors and 8 to 10 types of knowledge, skills, and attitudes required to deliver these critical behaviors. You want them to complete a high-level HILM to familiarize them with the tool and to jump-start their thinking on the topic.

Conducting the Meeting

For a more successful Rapid Design Team meeting, use both a scribe and a meeting facilitator. A junior curriculum developer is ideal for the scribe role. If you have virtual attendees, consider using web meeting technologies—such as the online meeting tool GoToMeeting (www.gotomeeting.com), which, it proclaims, "allows you to host an online meeting with up to 15 people—so you can do more and travel less." Select technologies that allow for real-time participation and viewing of documents.

Whenever possible, have your senior business leader sponsor kick off the meeting. Key messages include meeting outcomes and the expectations of the design team. In most cases, the program sponsor will not be able to attend the entire meeting. Arrange for a daily debriefing to ensure that the sponsor is engaged with the team meeting's progress, issues, and decisions.

As mentioned above, the HILM is the central framework for your Rapid Design Team meeting. Figure 4-16 gives an example showing the key elements of an HILM completed for a sales effectiveness and productivity learning program. In this case, the business leaders and Sales Council knew that to achieve their goals of higher profit margins and a more expansive revenue relationship with the customer, salespeople would need to increase their effectiveness and productivity.

All your supplier finalists *or* your internal learning developers will attend day 1 of the meeting to gain a deeper understanding of the business goals, business context, learning requirements, and learning preferences of the target audience. They will observe firsthand as the business leaders create the HILM. During day 1, each supplier finalist *or* your internal learning developer has an opportunity to ask further questions of the business leaders, learning function leaders, and sourcing team members, if applicable. To maintain equity, all supplier finalists remain in the meeting and are privy to the other supplier finalists' questions.

At the close of day 1, the supplier finalists *or* internal learning developers are given instructions for preparing their day 2 design presentation. Overnight, the suppliers *or* internal learning developers are busy creating their initial learning design.

For outsourced development, day 2 is made up of individual supplier presentations and supplier selection. Only one supplier at a time is allowed in the room to present, which ensures that there is no unfair advantage to their presentation order. Make sure to review the supplier selection matrix with the Rapid Design Team before the supplier presentations. A sample matrix is depicted in figure 4-17.

For internally developed learning, you will adapt this supplier presentation portion to include your internal learning developer's presentation of their recommended design. One technique is to have the recommended design mapped out on the walls. The internal learning

Figure 4-16. An Example of the Key Elements of a High Impact Learning Map

Sales Effectiveness and Productivity High-Impact Learning Map

Key KSAs	*Critical Behaviors*	*Key Results*	*Business Goals*
As a result of this program the participants will know.... • K1–How to build a territory plan • K2-The criteria for evaluating and segmenting customers • K3-How to develop territory quadrant travel maps • K4-Time management principles and how to apply to scheduling • K5-Effective phone skills to set confirm appointments • K6-Effective cold calling techniques qualify and set appointments • K7-How to build and manage pipeline activities • K8-How to develop accurate sales forecasts • K9-How to develop an annual customer strategic selling plan • K10-How to ask effective questions • K11-How to actively listen to customers • K12-How to explore, expand, respond to customers and overcome objections • K13-How to perform a market analysis to identify desirable channel partners that meet IR requirements • K14-How to develop an effective pre-call plan • K15-The key components, tools and process required to perform a customer needs analysis and conduct a planning meeting • K16-How to develop a channel partner business plan • K17-How to identify key decision makers and influencers • K18-How to identify different customer orientations and effective methods to interact with each type • K19-How to present with purpose • K20- How to develop and present customer proposals • K21-To follow up with customers • K22-How to gain access to C level executives • K23-How to perform competitive analysis	As a result of this program the participants will.... • CB1-Create and follow monthly territory plans • CB2-Prioritize customers into segmentation groups • CB3-Break territory into travel quadrants • CB4-Set and confirm customer appointments by phone • CB5-Cold call for new prospects • CB6-Manage time effectively to focus on value added activities and eliminate waste • CB7-Perform market analysis to identify new opportunities • CB8-Maintain a robust and balanced pipeline of revenue producing opportunities • CB9-Develop accurate sales forecasts • CB10-Develop pre-call plans for customer visits • CB11-Conduct customer needs analysis and planning meetings • CB12-Develop effective business plans with channel partners • CB13-Present solutions (not products) to customers • CB14-Implement effective questioning techniques that uncover customer needs, requirements, expectations and desired results • CB15-Actively listen to customers and present solutions that are aligned with customer needs, requirements, expectations • CB16-Embrace all customer responses to questions and proposals and explore and expand for additional information to respond and overcome objections • CB17-Identify key decision makers, influencers and blockers, increasing customer face time with the right people to ensure an IR win • CB18-Develop customized meeting strategies and presentations based on customer orientation • CB19-Initiate mutually beneficial relationships within customer organizations • CB20-Plan and deliver professional presentations, proposals and follow up documents • CB21-Meet with "C" level customers • CB22-Perform competitive analysis and align sales strategies with marketing plans	• KR1-Invoice to Pocket Price improvement of at least 1% • KR2-High profitability margin per sales employee range IR sales strategy • KR3-Measureable market share improvement in all legacy product platforms • KR4-Increase in forecast sales ratio of integrated solutions versus products • KR5-Increase in sales meetings with C Level customers yielding closed sales by minimum of 10%	• BG1-Increase pricing profit margins • BG3-Increased customer share of wallet • BG4-Increase recurring revenue

Source: Ingersoll Rand University, 2010.

Figure 4-17. Supplier Selection Matrix

Design Team Member Name

Scoring Scale-Rank each item below on a scale of 1-5 1 is ACCEPTABLE and 5 is EXCEPTIONAL		
	Presentation One	Presentation Two
SERVICE DELIVERY APPROACH	Supplier One	Supplier Two
Program accomplishes High Impact Learning Map learning specs		
Sales methodology and sales process aligned with our company solution sales needs		
Program layout and windowpane (flow of the program)		
Appropriate blend of learning techniques (presentation, activities, role play)		
Effective skill-building modules (sample of course work)		
Effective on-the-job sales tools and job aides		
Effective pre work and post work		
Global considerations addressed in design concept		
Supplier demonstrates leading edge sales subject matter expertise		
Proven record of results working with large organizations similar to IR		
Supplier ability to align course with additional Sales College Solution Sales Suite		
Depth of expert global facilitators with ability to handle high volume of deliveries		
SCORING TOTAL Comments/Recommendation		

Source: Ingersoll Rand University, 2010.

developer presents the design first. Following this, each Rapid Design Team member individually records design edits on Post-it Notes. As they finish editing their notes, they should place them near the corresponding section of the design. Once this is complete, conduct a walk-through of the design edits and create affinity clusters. Once the affinity clusters are complete, discuss the potential design edits. If necessary, to arrive at final design editing decisions, you can use multi-dot voting (in this type of voting, individuals vote on their priorities using a limited number of dot stickers, and then the votes are visibly compiled, revealing a ranking of items from highest to lowest based on the greatest to least number of votes per item).

Selecting the Learning Supplier

The step of having the learning supplier selected by the Rapid Design Team is for externally developed learning only. Once the suppliers complete their presentations, they will leave your meeting. This allows for candid discussion among team members regarding the supplier selection matrix results and other issues critical to supplier selection. In most cases, a decision will result. In a few cases, additional information may be requested from these suppliers and virtually shared with the team to aid in making a final supplier selection decision.

Once the supplier is identified, you need to communicate both to the winning supplier and to the other supplier candidates. Suppliers not chosen often ask for feedback on why they were not chosen. In the spirit of continuous improvement and future potential partnerships, you should provide basic feedback to these suppliers. An example of a communication to a supplier not selected appears in figure 4-18.

Figure 4-18. Follow-Up Email to Suppliers Not Selected

Place a personal call first, then follow up with email for record keeping purposes.

Dear ______________ :

It was good talking with you yesterday. Just wanted to follow up with an email on our conversation. Once again, thank you for attending our design meeting for the Sales Productivity program and submitting your proposal for the development and delivery of this curriculum. As I mentioned to you during our phone call, after listening to each of the proposal presentations, we realized that our decision was going to be difficult. We have, however, decided to go with another supplier. Although you were not chosen to support this particular project, it does not preclude us from utilizing you on potentially other future projects. Thanks again for all the time and effort you put into this initiative.

Best Regards,

Curriculum Program Manager

From Design to Development

Once your learning design is selected, you are ready to move to the development of the learning solution. It is important to review with your Rapid Design Team members their ongoing roles and responsibilities for the development stage of your new product development process. In the development stage of your learning solution, the primary role of your Rapid Design Team is as reviewers and approvers. They can also help you find content experts in the business. In addition, review with them the NPD project plan key development stages and decision gates:

- Indicate that the rapid design meeting is part of stage three—development—of the NPD project plan.
- Note key review and approval decision gates.
- Remind them that stage four of the NPD will involve testing and validation—in this case, their involvement in piloting learning programs.

In the NPD excerpt depicted in figure 4-19, note that the dark-colored cells highlight potential engagement points for Rapid Design Team members.

Engaging Leaders as Teachers

So far in this chapter, we have focused on engaging business leaders in the first two key learning activities: strategic governance and the design of learning solutions. The third key activity of learning functions is the deployment and delivery of your learning solutions, which you can best accomplish by engaging leaders in delivering your learning solutions—not only a powerful driver to create strategic alignment but also a boon for organizational and individual development. This approach, which is commonly referred to as "leaders teaching leaders" or "leaders as teachers," is a broad concept describing a variety of leadership engagement activities, including teaching, co-teaching, guest speaking, and postlearning program coaching.

The CorpU 10th Annual Benchmarking Study of Learning Excellence and Innovation, which studied more than 150 companies, estimates

Figure 4-19. Excerpt of Development Stage From Overall Design and Development Project Plan

	Task	Start Date	End Date	Duration	% Complete	Resource (Learning Managers, Sponsor, Rapid Design Team, Sourcing)
	Edits based on review					
	Alpha Test					
	Beta verification					
	Design Team Meeting – review of Beta					
	Beta test					
	Additional tests, key targeted segments (HR, IT, etc.)					
	Final Sign Off					
	Develop Story Board MIB					
	Internal Review of MIB Storyboard					
	Design Team and SME review of storyboards					
	Compile feedback and send to Vendor					
	Update storyboard with company feedback					
	Alpha review – Learning Luncheon "Early" Review					
	Feedback to Supplier					
	Alpha Review					
	Edits based on review					
	Alpha Test					
	Beta Review					
	Design Team Meeting – review of Beta					
	Beta Test					
	Additional testers, key targeted segments (HR, IT, etc.)					
	Sign Off					
	Develop Program Materials					
	Develop Facilitator Materials					
	Receive Phase Gate 3 Approval					
	Phase Gate 4 – Testing and Validation					
	Pilot WBT					
	Revise materials as needed					
	Pilot ILT/Meeting in a Box					
	Revise Materials as needed					
	Qualitative/Quantitative Report					

	Task	Start Date	End Date	Duration	% Complete	Resource (Learning Managers, Sponsor, Rapid Design Team, Sourcing)
	Compile feedback and update objectives/requirements for vendor					
	RFP, Select Vendor					
	Create CES, get approval, and sign Vendor agreement					
	Submit PO request (CES)					
	Create Master Service Agreement					
	Finalize Contract					
	Initial Supplier design meeting					
	Supplier Integration Form					
	Develop Deployment Plan					
	Send Key Facts Sheet to VP Enterprise Learning and EL team					
	Receive Phase Gate 2 approval					
	Phase Gate 30 – Development					
	Create Detailed Project Plan					
	Create Instruction Design Document					
	Determine reporting requirements & communicate to technology department					
	Develop Evaluation Plan					
	Develop Story Board WBT (Web based training)					
	Internal review of WBT storyboard					
	Design Team SME review of storyboards					
	Compile feedback & send to Supplier					
	Update storyboard with company feedback					
	Content Outline event					
	Finalize Course Outline					
	Functionally Test Checklist					
	Visual Storyboard Review					
	Feedback to Supplier					
	Approve Final Materials					
	Confirm Deployment Schedule					
	Translations					
	Receive approval ignore from reviewer					
	Final Sign off					
	Communication Plan					
	Final Deployment Plan Approval					
	After Action Review					
	Executive Briefing					
	Delivery Schedule					
	Update Learning Program Website					
	Program Evaluation					
	Post Launch Design Team Meeting					

that approximately 35 percent of these organizations engage leaders in teaching leadership programs and 28 percent in teaching for nonleadership programs. Organizations such as General Electric, PepsiCo, BD, Colgate-Palmolive, Procter & Gamble, 3M, and Intel are pioneers and role models for incorporating leaders as teachers into their learning strategies. Although these are large Fortune 500 firms, smaller organizations also can and do engage leaders as teachers. Ed Betof's seminal book on this topic, *Leaders as Teachers: Unlock the Teaching Potential of Your Company's Best and Brightest* (2009), provides a detailed approach to creating a leaders-as-teachers program that can be tailored to organizations of all sizes.

The Benefits of Engaging Leaders as Teachers

As the world economy continues to move from being industry based to knowledge based, companies are increasingly aspiring to become true teaching organizations. In a teaching organization, everyone is a teacher and everyone is a learner. In a rapidly changing, competitive global marketplace, speed to market is paramount. Global competitors can quickly replicate a successful new product. However, they cannot quickly replicate an organization's intellectual capital. The speed of knowledge transfer and shared learning become a company's competitive differentiator in a global market. In *The Cycle of Leadership: How Great Leaders Teach Their Companies to Win*, Noel Tichy and Nancy Cardwell (2004) describe this as a "virtuous teaching cycle." In the "virtuous teaching cycle," both the learner and the leader as teacher experience mutual, interactive learning. The leader as teacher develops a teachable point of view and is informed by the learner's viewpoint and experiences. Likewise, the learner benefits from the leader as teacher's point of view and experiences.

In the context of a teaching organization, leaders as teachers are an important lever for knowledge transfer and shared learning. In Betof's *Leaders as Teachers*, a number of business benefits derived from leaders serving as teachers are discussed. The following list of business benefits is inspired by Betof's work on the value of leaders as teachers:

- Drives common messages for change across the organization.
- Creates two-way, reciprocal learning.

- Provides platform for exposure to talent within the organization.
- Improves the leadership skills of those who teach.
- Increases the levels of employee engagement.
- Communicates that learning is valued by the organization.

With these principles in mind, let's look at some of the ways in which leaders serving as teachers can strengthen the learning function. Leaders can serve as instructors, coaches, on expert panels, and in a host other teaching roles. For the sake of brevity, here I focus on a leaders-as-teachers process that is more informal and creates more personal connections between the leader and students. I've chosen a particular program that embodies these principles with which I'm very familiar, Ingersoll Rand's Visiting Executive Program. This branded program is modeled after a style of dialogue known as the "fireside chat," which is useful to consider in some detail.

Creating "Fireside Chats" with the Visiting Executive Program

There are many excellent resources, such as Betof's book, that provide road maps for using leaders as faculty in your learning programs. However, the focus in this chapter is on a highly successful, scalable, and relatively easy-to-implement guest speaker role for leaders as teachers. This guest-speaking role is the key feature of the Visiting Executive Program—as it is branded by Ingersoll Rand—which is unique in the level of intimacy, informality, reflective insight, and customized, relevant messages that it provides.

The Visiting Executive Program is similar to the "fireside chats" used so successfully by U.S. president Franklin Delano Roosevelt during the Great Depression of the 1930s and World War II in the 1940s. Via radio broadcasts, FDR spoke in intimate and conversational tones with the entire nation. In response to his fireside chats, millions of letters were sent to the White House expressing renewed hope, confidence in the recovery plan (the New Deal), and unity in the face of that time's economic troubles (see Mankowski and Raissa, 2003).

The Great Depression was a time of much suffering and uncertainty for America. When FDR gave his first fireside chat in 1933, more than one-third of the workforce was unemployed and every bank had been closed for eight days. He crafted his communication to be brief (15–45 minutes), and he used basic language and stories to explain complex financial recovery issues facing the country. In explaining complicated New Deal issues, he used a simple baseball analogy. He spoke in terms of "we" instead of "you." He invited the American people to "tell me your troubles." All 31 of FDR's fireside chats are available through the Museum of Broadcast Communications (www.museum.tv), offering a deeper understanding of FDR's authentic communication and leadership style.

The Visiting Executive Program promotes authentic communication for leaders. It is a vast departure from a formal guest speaker presentation using multiple slides. In fact, there is one rule: "no slides." Leaders who serve as visiting executives relinquish their prepared slide presentations to create a direct, informal dialogue with learning participants. Of course, some leaders balk at giving up their slide presentation security blanket. But with your help and support, they will grow comfortable with their fireside chats with learning participants. They will actually get quite good at this. In fact, participants consistently rate the visiting executive portion of learning programs as the high point. Similarly, the leaders participate again and again as visiting executives and report its high value in return for the time invested.

The Visiting Executive's Purpose

A program like one for visiting executives deeply engages leaders in learning. In addition, the visiting executive enhances the relevance of the learning by linking the business to the learning content. Ultimately, the overriding purpose is to engage leaders in creating better alignment between learning and business priorities. In the process, there are also other benefits, such as leadership development, business relevance, and exposure to talent. From a developmental perspective, the visiting executive role helps leaders craft what Noel Tichy refers to as their "teachable point of view," which he defines as a cohesive set of ideas, values, and ways of energizing people that can be put into action. This is based on the premise that in order to teach, a leader *must* have a teachable point of view, which has four key elements:

- Ideas: How does your business make money and win in the marketplace?
- Values: What behaviors are required to put your business ideas into practice?
- Emotional energy: How do you keep people motivated and working with high energy?
- Edge: Which difficult decisions must be made?

In addition to these four elements, a successful teachable point of view is best communicated in a storytelling mode, which integrates ideas, values, and emotional energy and edge with one, two, or all three storylines. In *Leading Minds*, Howard Gardner (1996) points out that humans learn through stories. In studying successful leaders, he found that three basic storylines were most common:

- *Who am I?*—personal stories that explain how the life experiences have shaped the leader and his or her point of view.
- *Who are we?*—stories that demonstrate how joint experiences, attitudes, and beliefs of the group form a shared point of view.
- *Where are we going?*—stories that capture the necessity of change and excitement concerning the future direction of the group.

Most important, the visiting executive should develop his or her own teachable point of view. Self-reflection during the creation process generates authentic messaging. Like FDR's fireside chats, the message should be easily understood and concise.

Creating a Sustainable Visiting Executive Process

At this point, some of you may be thinking that although the Visiting Executive Program is a good concept, in the past you have experienced issues with executives honoring their commitment as guest speakers. In many organizations, this experience of last-minute cancellations or no-shows is common. However, a few companies do have a 100 percent visiting executive commitment rate. There is no magic here; the difference is creating a business process that will ensure that the visiting executive is effective and sustainable for the organization (see the sidebar).

Figure 4-20 provides an overview of the Visiting Executive Program for the learning leader that contains many of the process elements described above. Specifically, the document addresses purpose, role/responsibilities, selection, and support materials available. The learning leader leverages portions of this overview document, such as roles and responsibilities, to communicate with the visiting executive population.

The program's process itself drives accountability for leaders to honor their visiting executive commitments. If a rare, urgent business matter creates a conflict for the visiting executive, this is already accounted for and rectified by the process. In contracting with the visiting executive, they must partner with the staff managing the learning function to iden-

The Business Process for the Visiting Executive Program

Mandatory elements of the Visiting Executive Program business process include

- Charter (program purpose) supported by senior leaders.
- Contract providing clear roles, responsibilities, and expectations.
- A design that is scalable.
- Goals and metrics for the program.
- A repeatable mechanism to identify a pool of visiting executives.
- An annual scheduling process aligned with business leaders' schedules.
- Preprogram briefing conversation with visiting executive.
- User-friendly briefing materials to assist the visiting executive.
- Ongoing feedback and development provided for visiting executive effectiveness.
- Tracking and reporting for the program.
- Reward/recognition for visiting executive participation.

tify and secure their emergency replacement. In effect, the replacement visiting executive participates in the process as an understudy.

Setting measurable goals, tracking, and reporting on this performance capture the attention of business leaders. Tracking participation levels by business unit, geographies, functions, and so on gives transparency to the process and generates accountability.

Leveraging and publicizing your most senior leaders as visible role models in the Visiting Executive Program sends a powerful message to business leaders across the organization. If the CEO can lead a visiting exccutive session without cancellation, surely other leaders can find similar time.

Figure 4-20. An Overview of a Visiting Executive Program

Program Purpose	The Visiting Executive program with the Corporate University was developed to • Provide visible leadership support for the Company's commitment to developing talent • Give executives exposure to the talent within the Company, become more familiar with the program's purpose, and better understand the business issues the participants encounter. • Give employees greater exposure to the Company's senior leaders and learn about the business directly from the leaders
Visiting Executive's Messages	Key messages the visiting executive should share with the program participants include • Background on themselves and connection with the Corporate University, if any • Their personal leadership perspective • Importance of the program • Relevant experiences regarding the program's content • Getting the most out of the learning experience • Answer questions on business issues
Goal	In 2009 our is goal to have • 100% of all programs have a Visiting Executive • 25% of the senior executives one and two levels from CEO will have served as a Visiting Executive of the Corporate University program
Identification of Leaders	The identification of Visiting Executives should be the joint responsibility between the program owner and the deployment representative. On a regular basis (yearly, quarterly, etc.) the deployment representative identifies a pool of executives to address the Company owned and deployed programs; whereas the program owner identifies executives for programs that require a representative from a specific functional area. Executives can be identified through several venues including • Self-Nomination • Organization Leadership Reviews (OLR) • Key stakeholder groups such as Human Resources, Talent and Organizational Development, Enterprise Focus Area teams, Functional Councils, Functional Leaders, etc. • Expectations set by the CEO

Roles and Responsibilities

The successful deployment of the program requires the collaboration of three groups of people within the company including the program owner, the corporate University deployment representative, and executive. The following table highlights the responsibilities of each group

	Program Owner Curriculum manager or Regional representative	**Deployment** ESA, AP, and Americas	**Waiting Executives**
Pre	• Update "Visiting Executive Course Briefing" document (as needed) • Identify existing executive for each program under their curriculum area that require a representative from a specific functional area • In partnership with the Corporate University regional deployment representative, brief executives on roles and responsibilities prior to program date • Prepare key messages to xxx visiting Executive portion of the program	• Identify pool of visiting Executives • Confirm visiting Executives attendance and distribute program information • Provide visiting Executive background information to program owner • In partnership with the Corporate University program owner, brief executive on roles and responsibilities prior to program date • Inform Visiting Executive of any program or logistic changes • Reserve room or area for Visiting Executive session • Prepare for Visiting Executive virtual delivery (if needed)	• Review "Visiting Executive Course Briefing" document • Meet with program owner to review roles and responsibilities • Prepare for 15-30 minute talk
During	• Orchestrate Visiting Executive session	• Prepare room for Visiting Executive session • Serve as on-site contact for Visiting Executive during session	• Present to program participants and conduct Q&A • Attend group dinner (if possible)
Post	• Send follow-up thank-you and evaluation results to visiting executive • In partnership with the Corporate University regional deployment representative, follow-up with executive on evaluation results	• Update and track visiting executive participation • In partnership with the Corporate University program owner, follow-up with executive on evaluation results	• Review program evaluations and seek feedback from program owner (improvement is needed)

Location	The best way to engage executives in the learning process is to have them attend the program and interact with the participants in person. There are a variety of reasons why this may not always be feasible or cost effective. For example: • The Corporate University is moving to a more distributed delivery model where we are "taking the learning closer to the learner" and a pool of executives may not be available in some locations. • The executive is traveling on business and will not return until the program has ended. • Traveling to the program location for the sole purpose of conducting the Visiting Executive portion does not justify the cost. To accommodate all situations the Corporate University will continue to encourage executives to attend the program in person. When this option is not feasible, cost-effective or possible a virtual delivery option will be provided. In 2009, the Corporate University will pilot use of "Live Meeting" to enable the visiting executives to participate virtually.
Support Materials	A variety of materials have been created to support the Corporate University's Visiting Executive program. These materials include • Identification of responsibilities and tasks associated with the program during the post phases of the Visiting Executive session (Program Owner, Deployment, Visiting Executive) • Communication templates – Memo to solicit a pool of participants – Pre-program invite to executive (Logistics, Program Background, their role, etc.) – Visiting Executive confirmation and preparation materials (Course Briefing, program roster, logistics, etc.) – Post-program thank-you notes – Visiting Executive evaluation results • Virtual "Live Meeting" instructions (visiting executive, facilitator)

To ensure that you have a scalable pool of visiting executives, target appropriate levels of leaders from various geographies. To manage travel costs, every attempt should be made to leverage the visiting executive in his or her regional geography or leverage a scheduled trip to another region. In the example given in figure 4-20, the targeted visiting executive pool is made up of 25 percent senior executives who are one and two levels down from the CEO. At Ingersoll Rand, each year there are about 90 visiting executive sessions across the globe. Many visiting executives request to participate in multiple sessions.

Finally, arranging for visiting executive sessions on an annual basis, in alignment with the business calendar, provides the necessary lead time for scheduling. Typically, the visiting executive is offered a choice of sessions. The operative word here is "choice," which gives them a sense of control and accountability for their selection of a participation date.

Visiting executive sessions can be held virtually or remotely using current collaborative technologies. However, face-to-face sessions are optimal.

Preparing Your Visiting Executive

When preparing your visiting executives, there are two important things to always keep in mind: Time is money for your business leaders and, despite their powerful roles, most of your business leaders are apprehensive of failing in front of others in their fireside chats. Armed with this knowledge, you can create a process and tools that conveniently, concisely, and quickly brief your visiting executives for their success.

Once your visiting executive is confirmed for a session, send the visiting executive a course briefing document, which provides specific learning outcomes, instructional methods used, target audience description, and a "windowpane" illustrating the entire course agenda. In addition, the document should give suggestions for key messaging points. Follow up with a conversation to answer questions, review logistics, help prepare the executive's message, review the course and participants, and allay his or her concerns. Typically, the visiting executive's understudy participates in this briefing. Figure 4-21 depicts an example of a visiting executive course briefing document. For additional context, the briefing can also include a conversation with the course instructor. Moreover, soliciting and compiling potential questions from course participants can be helpful in directing the visiting executive as to what is top of mind for the participants.

Evaluation Feedback for the Continual Development of Visiting Executives

One goal of the Visiting Executive Program is developing the leadership skills of the leaders who teach. Providing feedback from your observations as well as from course participants is helpful. Given the achievement orientation of most senior leaders, it does not surprise me when a visiting executive anxiously awaits feedback on his or her session. They often ask how their performance calibrates with those of other visiting executives. Figure 4-22 illustrates the specific participant evaluation questions regarding the visiting executive and the summary of his or her evaluation results. The best practice is to debrief the results with the visiting executive.

Figure 4-21. An Example of a Visiting Executive Course Briefing Document

Ingersoll Rand University
Visiting Executive
Course Briefing

Containing:

- Program Description
- Program Agenda
- Recommended Leadership Messaging

Program: **Leader Business Management**
IRU Contact:

Ingersoll Rand University

Leader Business Management

Overview

This course provides participants with a hands-on experience managing a simulated business, a review and application of common Ingersoll-Rand financial measures, and an opportunity to learn and network with other IR business leaders.

Primary Competencies Developed

- Business Driver
- Business Contributor
- Implementation Driver

The business simulation requires participants to think beyond their functional roles and act as general managers of the business, while working together to leverage resources to maximize results. Participants will develop their understanding of the key business levers that drive results in a competitive marketplace.

The topics covered in Leader Business Management include

- What the CEO Wants You to Know
- Developing Business Acumen
- Business Sheet: P&L
- Gross Profit
- Operating Cash Flow
- ROIC & CAGR
- SWOT Analyses
- ROA and ROE

Learning Outcomes

Upon completion of this 3-day course, participants will be able to

- Understand the key levers that drive business results
- Understand the reasons behind management decisions and strategic initiatives
- Think and act beyond their functional expertise to understand the business from multiple perspectives including sales, manufacturing, management, research and development, human resources, investors, and customers
- Make on-the-job business decisions based on a big picture view of the business
- Interpret and utilize common IR financial measures and basic principles of finance
- Enhance their personal impact on IR's performance by making informed decisions with a broader view of the business

Instructional Methods

This course primarily utilizes simulation, role play, and case study to maximize learning effectiveness for this content. The course is facilitated by one external IRU faculty member and requires completion of pre-work.

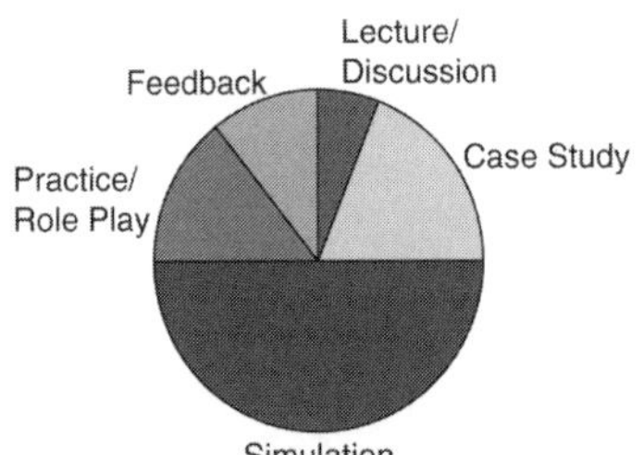

Target Audience

Leader Business Management is designed for high-performing individual contributors and managers in salary grades 27-30 that influence business and financial outcomes. Candidates will have at least 18 months with IR, and include plant managers, marketing managers, sales managers, human resource managers, initiative leaders, and managers of key projects or processes. Individuals who anticipate having P&L responsibility in the near future may benefit the most from this course.

IR Ingersoll Rand

Leader Business Management – Program Agenda

Day One DOOR International Faculty Ingersoll Rand Visiting Executive	**Day Two** DOOR International Faculty	**Day Three** DOOR International Faculty
8:00 am – 8:45 am **Welcome and Course Introduction** 8:45 am – 12:00 pm **DecisionBase Simulation Years 1 and 2** 12:00 pm – 1:00 pm **Lunch** 1:00 pm – 4:00 pm **DecisionBase Simulation Years 3 and 4** 5:00 pm – 6:00 pm **Visiting Executive Discussion** 6:00 pm – 7:30 pm **Reception and Dinner**	8:00 am – 12:00 pm **DecisionBase Simulation Years 5 – 8** 12:00 pm – 1:00 pm **Lunch** 1:00 pm – 2:00 pm **DecisionBase Simulation Years 5 – 8** 2:00 pm – 5:00 pm **IR-specific Application Exercises**	8:00 am – 12:00 pm **Rufus Company Case Study** Analyze Case, Develop SWOT Define Issues to Attack, Define Impact Of Issues on Group/Company 12:00 pm – 1:00 pm **Working Lunch** Prepare Presentation 1:00 pm – 3:30 pm **Group Presentations by Business Function** Present Business Case for Solution 3:30 – 4:00 pm **Wrap Up and Close**

Ingersoll Rand

Leader Business Management – Suggestions for Leadership Messaging

For Visiting Executive Role:

- If a Strategy Board Member, mention your governance role for Ingersoll Rand
- Leadership Education and the building of Strategic Organizational Competencies through Ingersoll Rand University
- Highlight your visit as having multiple purpose: to experience the Ingersoll Rand University "product", better understand the business issues the participants encounter, and to provide visible leadership support for Ingersoll Rand's commitment to developing talent
- NO SLIDES, please.........the participants just want to hear your views on how this particular program aligns with IR strategy
- Approximately 30 minutes is ample. Please allow time for and encourage questions.
- Attend the group's evening dinner for some great interaction with the participants.

Key Messaging to Support Course Content/Objectives:

Share a personal story that illustrates how business acumen capabilities have aided you in managing a business, business unit, or project. The right story about you can be the best way to connect to the group. And the right story about your use of this skill can be the best way to reinforce the importance of what they are learning.

Ingersoll Rand continues its aggressive pursuit to create organic growth in a global diversified industrial environment. With this in mind, the company has a critical need to develop Leaders, Managers, and Individual Contributors with strong people and business management skills. Globally, these high-potential and high-performing individuals, with respect to business acumen, must

- understand the fundamental drivers of business success
- be able to make sound business decisions after taking into account short- versus long-term tradeoffs, as well as strategic, financial, operational/cross-functional, competitive, economic, and interpersonal issues.
- be able to operationalize Ingersoll Rand's vision, by understanding how they can drive Dramatic Growth, Operational Excellence, and Dual Citizenship in their businesses.

Building global bench strength is an essential enabler to achieving Ingersoll Rand's growth strategy and ensuring organizational success. Leadership and General Management competencies were developed to identify the behaviors and skill sets Ingersoll Rand requires to execute its global strategy. Leader Business Management is one of the educational/developmental levers to achieving such success.

The Leader Business Management program resides within the IRU Leadership and General Management College. This program, branded separately as Business Acumen, is available to the IR businesses as a Course-on-Location, meaning it can be taught at a business site. Currently, this program is IRU's most sought after program for both IRU location attendance and as a Course-on-Location offering.

Figure 4-22. Visiting Executive Program Evaluation Questions

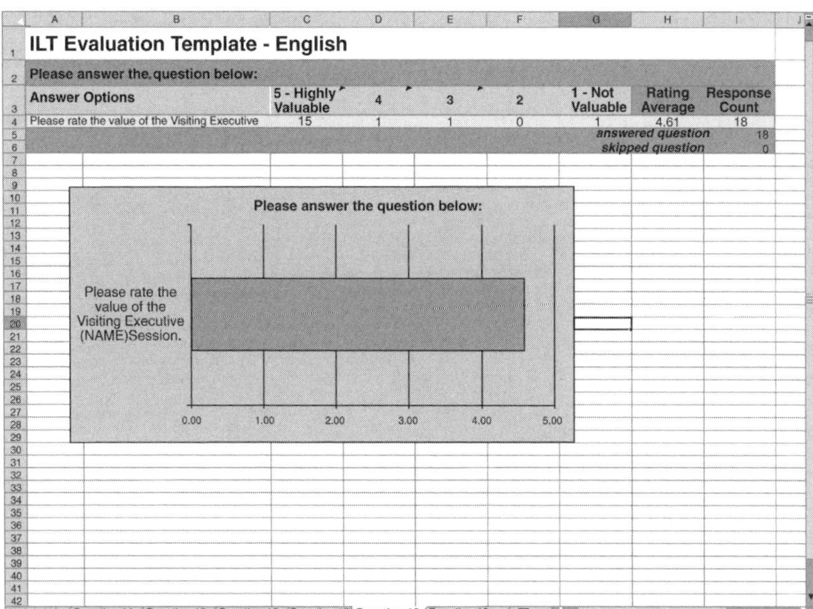

ILT Evaluation Template - English

Please answer the question below:							
Answer Options	**5 - Highly Valuable**	**4**	**3**	**2**	**1 - Not Valuable**	**Rating Average**	**Response Count**
Please rate the value of the Visiting Executive	15	1	1	0	1	4.61	18
						answered question	18
						skipped question	0

ILT Evaluation Template - English

How did the Visiting Executive session impact your experience?		
Answer Options		**Response Count**
		13
	answered question	13
	skipped question	5
Number	**Response Date**	**Response Text**
1	Aug 18, 2009 2:44 PM	Liked how he kept it real
2	Aug 18, 2009 2:57 PM	good insight to business
3	Aug 18, 2009 2:59 PM	Nice to know leaders struggle with same issues
4	Aug 18, 2009 3:58 PM	Valuable
5	Aug 18, 2009 4:27 PM	Q&A was very informal and open
6	Aug 19, 2009 12:07 PM	N/A
7	Aug 19, 2009 12:25 PM	nice to meet him
8	Aug 19, 2009 12:32 PM	Interesting to see it relate back to company
9	Aug 19, 2009 12:32 PM	Q&A was valuable
10	Aug 19, 2009 12:38 PM	Great learning
11	Aug 19, 2009 12:40 PM	Related our company values and strategic objectives to the course objectives in a practical way.
12	Aug 19, 2009 4:45 PM	Learned about the strategy behind our targeting the new markets
13	Aug 19, 2009 6:32 PM	Liked the questions he asked us

Question 14 / Question 15 / Question 16 / Question 17 / Question 18 / **Question 19**

Recognizing Visiting Executive Participation

There are a number of ways to recognize your visiting executive's participation. Here are a few proven approaches:

- Placing a photo from the session and a focus story in your company's main employee communication media.
- Publishing an annual Hall of Fame listing of your active visiting executives.
- Creating a physical visiting executives' Hall of Fame in your learning centers.
- Sending a framed photo from the visiting executive session.
- Sending a thank-you communication signed by the entire group of course participants for the visiting executive session.
- Sending a thank-you communication to the visiting executive from your CEO.
- Listing visiting executive participants in talent review discussions and documentation.

Different approaches will work for your particular company. The important thing is to include recognition as a key part of your visiting executive process.

Key Points for Governing the Learning Function

- To drive transparency and business leader engagement, engage your leaders in learning governance.
- Set up different levels of learning governance to drive strategy, curriculum content/delivery, and learning operations.
- Use a governance charter to ensure clarity on roles/responsibilities and membership criteria.
- Recognize leaders serving on your governance boards.

An Exercise on Governing the Learning Function

Select one of your existing learning governance bodies. Using the sample representation list below, place a check mark next to the membership team representation you believe is critical to the success of this learning governance body. Now review the actual membership team for this governance body. What gaps exist, and how will you close them? If you currently have no learning governance in place, apply this exercise to a governance body you plan to create.

Sample Representation List for a Learning Governance Team
Senior HR leader
Highest levels of senior leadership
All key business units
Multiple geographies or regions
A resistant leader or two
A majority of senior leaders who are passionate supporters of learning
Functional expert (such as engineering, information technology)
Senior leader(s) of your company's strategic business initiative(s)
External thought leader
Midlevel, high potential leader for a development opportunity
Key external supplier
Other: ______________________________

Key Points for Designing and Developing Learning Solutions

- The design and development of new learning solutions is very similar to the development stage of new product development processes used by businesses.
- A growing trend for businesses in their NPD processes is collaborating with customers, suppliers, and other stakeholders to co-design and develop new products.
- Using a Rapid Design Team process, this collaborative approach can successfully be applied to the design and development of new learning solutions.
- By engaging business leaders, suppliers, and other stakeholders as co-designers of your learning solutions, you will achieve

increasingly relevant learning, align learning with business priorities, and strengthen leaders' ownership of the learning.

- The High Impact Learning Map, which creates a direct connection between business results and learning, is the framework for the Rapid Design Team meeting.

Exercise on Designing and Developing Learning Solutions

Using the Stage Gate NPD process as a model for the development of your learning solutions, identify how your business leaders, suppliers, and key stakeholders are currently engaged in the development, testing and validation, launch, and postlaunch review stages. Are there gaps to close?

Key Points on Engaging Leaders as Teachers

- The leaders-as-teachers process engages your business leaders to create a more agile and competitive teaching organization.
- There are many business benefits from a leaders-as-teachers initiative, including developing the leadership skills of those who teach.
- One powerful leaders-as-teachers method is the guest speaker fireside chat, which gives leaders an intimate and highly relevant way to converse with course participants. At Ingersoll Rand, this method is branded the Visiting Executive Program.
- The success of a Visiting Executive Program is directly related to its management as a *business process*.
- Make sure that participation in your Visiting Executive Program is easy, successful, and desirable for your business leaders.

Exercises on Engaging Leaders as Teachers

1. For each of the stakeholder audiences listed below, list your key "selling" points for deploying a visiting executive–type program in your organization.

CEO ____
CFO ____
Senior HR leader ____
Senior leaders ____
Potential visiting executives _______________________________
Learning professionals ____________________________________
Course teacher or facilitator ______________________________
Course participants ______________________________________

2. Using the list below, indicate which elements are currently used in your guest-speaking programs. Where is there opportunity for you? Mandatory elements of the Visiting Executive Program business process include:

____ Charter (program purpose) supported by senior leaders.
____ Contract providing clear roles, responsibilities, and expectations.
____ A design that is scalable.
____ Goals and metrics for the program.
____ A repeatable mechanism to identify a pool of the visiting executive.
____ An annual scheduling process aligned with business leaders' schedules.
____ Preprogram briefing conversation with the visiting executive.
____ User-friendly briefing materials to assist the visiting executive.
____ Ongoing feedback and development provided for the visiting executive's effectiveness.
____ Tracking and reporting for the program.
____ Reward/recognition for visiting executives' participation.

If you do not currently have a guest-speaking program like visiting executives in place, rate the ease (high, medium, low) of implementing each element in your organization. How will this rating inform the design for your guest-speaking process?

Chapter 5

Communicating Your Business Results

What's in this chapter:

- How to create a strategic communication plan for your learning function.
- How to craft your targeted communication in the language of business.
- How to use external communication to build the reputation of your learning solutions.

■ ■ ■

As we have seen in the first four chapters, the Strategic Learning Alignment Model provides a system of four steps to help you create powerful alignment with your business leaders. Step 4, *Communicating Your Business Results*, draws from and supports your efforts from the previous three steps—*Knowing Your Business*, *Building the Business Case for Learning*, and *Engaging Leaders in Key Learning Activities*.

To drive engagement and the alignment that follows, your business leaders need to be continually aware of the effectiveness and efficiency of your learning function. On a daily basis, your business leaders and other key stakeholders are bombarded by enormous amounts of data, information, and messaging. In fact, the Radicati Group, a communication research company, estimates that worldwide by 2013, more than 500 billion email messages will be sent daily. Your challenge is to break through this communication overload to engage your business leaders with your learning function.

Throughout out this book, I advocate a systematic approach to creating alignment with your key stakeholders. I similarly recommend an integrated communication system to strengthen your business leaders' engagement—"mindshare"—with learning. An integrated communication system for learning involves planning and managing all aspects of your communication with key stakeholders. This includes marketing communication for a new learning solution, reinforcing your learning "brand," publicizing external recognition, and reporting on learning's effectiveness and efficiency. Rather than have communication be event based and fragmented, a systematic approach allows you to use your communication efforts more strategically. Your communication system becomes a major lever to drive leader engagement and alignment with your learning.

Business leaders are familiar with communications strategies. In fact, businesses use communications to build brand reputation, market their products and services, and engage their employees and other key stakeholders. In fact, many companies have a dedicated corporate communications function to manage their integrated communications strategy. Once again, we can borrow from established processes and tools already used by our business and apply them in our communication strategy.

There are two overall categories of business communications, internal and external. Internal communications primarily consists of employee communication. External communication is typically targeted to stakeholders outside the organization. External communication includes marketing, brand management, customer relations, and public relations (publicity). Your learning function has three key components of external communication: reputation, brand, customers, and opportunities for external recognition. By borrowing from the processes and tools of both internal and external communication, learning professionals can build strong alignment with their business.

In their 2007 book *Essentials of Corporate Communication Implmenting Practices for Effective Reputation Management*, Cees van Riel and Charles Fombrun of the Reputation Institute discuss Coca-Cola as an example of a company using an integrated approach to communications. Coca-Cola's business strategy is to offer consumers more than 300 product choices to meet individual preferences and to make the product highly accessible—literally within "an arm's length of thirst," and at an affordable price for its value. The local bottling system allows the company to operate close to its global customers and communities. The Coca-Cola brand is synonymous with quality and enjoyment.

Coca-Cola's external communication highlights the consistent quality and enjoyment of its products. Its messaging emphasizes the many product choices available to consumers. In addition, Coca-Cola often gains publicity by frequently sponsoring local community sporting and festival events. As part of local communities, the company also communicates its sustainability efforts. In an effort to keep close to customer preferences, feedback in the voices of their customers is regularly collected. Each month, Coca-Cola tests 20 brand attributes with 4,000 consumers to measure movement. Thus, its business strategy guides an integrated approach to communications (van Riel and Charles Fombrun 2007, 175–76).

This same type of integrated communications strategy also applies to your learning function. As with any strategy, a plan defining your audiences, key messages, timing, and choice of communication method will guide your communications implementation throughout the year.

Creating a Strategic Communication Plan for Your Learning

A strategic communication plan for your learning function describes your key strategic messaging objectives, target audiences, communication vehicles, frequency, timing, responsible members of your team, and expected outcomes. It is important here to differentiate a *strategic* communication plan from an operational communication plan. A strategic communication plan is derived directly from the learning function's strategies. It includes the overarching strategic messaging you want to communicate with your stakeholders. It provides a big-picture view of your overall strategic communication, which allows you to optimize timing and targeted audiences to increase alignment with the business.

An operational communication plan, in contrast, is more events based and tactical. Examples of operational communication are messages used to announce enrollment for a learning program or completion requirements for a compliance program. Although this level of communication is important to your learning function, here we are focusing on strategic communication to create alignment of your learning with the business.

An annual, strategic communication plan provides the communications road map with which you can engage your key internal and external stakeholders. Without such a road map, you risk fragmented communications—your efforts to communicate are suboptimal. Consequently, you are expending effort on communications with little return for your learning function. This is a common challenge for learning professionals. A 2008 Expertus, Inc., study found that only 15 percent of learning functions surveyed have an internal marketing plan in place. And of those with plans, only 60 percent include measures of its effectiveness.

Now let's look at a case example of a strategic communication plan. (The case examples given throughout this chapter are actual strategic communications used by a corporate university.)

Case Background for a Strategic Communication Plan

The strategic communication plan for this corporate university has been carefully articulated. Given that the learning strategy drives the communication plan, it is important to note that this strategy:

- Develops a global leadership pipeline.
- Develops strategic capabilities, such as solution-selling expertise.
- Drives one company culture across the organization.
- Offers practical learning solutions embedded into the work.
- Engages leaders in learning.
- Runs the learning function as a business process.

The "brand," or identity, of this corporate university is summarized by its brand slogan—Link, Leverage, and Learn.

An Annual Strategic Communication Plan

Let's consider a particular example of an annual strategic communication plan for learning, shown in figure 5-1. The excerpt of the plan matrix given in the figure details two of the corporate university's strategic messages integrated into a communication plan.

Before we look at figure 5-1 in more detail, in general, your annual strategic communication plan should include

- the message
- your purpose—whether it is to inform, persuade, or remind
- method—of communication, such as video or testimonials
- timing
- effectiveness metric for communication, or how you will measure your communication's success in meeting your objectives
- owner—to ensure clarity and accountability
- target audience—the intended audience for the message, typically segmented populations.

Now, moving from left to right across the matrix given in figure 5-1, the first column contains the strategic message, and the third column shows the communication method. Your target audience and message type will guide your selection of a communication method. Figure 5-1 shows the communication methods selected to announce a new sales school to a target audience of salespeople. Given that salespeople are more relational in nature, a 30-second streaming video testimonial on the company's daily news website was selected. Also, brief testimonial endorsements from sales leaders and pilot class participants were used.

In developing the strategic communication plan, also consider additional factors such as global cultural differences, appropriate localization of your message, and variations in technology if you are communicating across the globe. You need to know in advance and create an alternate plan if, for example, the technology in an emerging global market cannot support streaming video technology. Likewise, ensure that the content of your message is understandable by global audiences. You should

Figure 5-1. Sample Excerpt From an Annual Strategic Communication Plan for Learning

Message	Purpose	Method	Timing	Effectiveness Metric for Communication	Owner	Target audience:	Strategy Board	Sr. Leaders	Mid-level leaders	HR Leaders	Sales People	Sales Leaders	General Population
Progress on filling the leadership pipeline	Inform	• Executive briefing - Metric Scoreboard	Mid-Year & End of Year	Awareness Demonstrated use Pipeline Internal Fills Data saved in latest reviews by business leaders	John		X	X	X	X		X	
Launch of Strategic Sales School	Inform	• Article in Company Daily E-News • Letter from executive sponsor to sales leaders	Pre-launch	Awareness survey results greater than 10% of sales community	Kim		X	X	X	X	X	X	X
	Purpose	• RSS sharing prior testimonials • Streaming videos of external sales expert Instructions on front page of Daily E-news	Launch	Enrollment @ 85% + utilities If searches on Sales School websites	Kim						X	X	
	Remind	• Participant testimonials of school's values	Monthly		Kim						X	X	

leverage global contacts to provide you with the necessary feedback on this.

As we continue to move across the matrix shown in figure 5-1, timing is next. The purpose for your communications—whether to inform, to persuade, to act, or to remind—influences your timing. In figure 5-1, a monthly timeframe was selected to remind the target sales audience of the new sales school.

You should time your communication to align with your company's business cycle and also for when it will be most useful for your target audience. For example, if development planning is emphasized in the first quarter of the year, you should align the timing of your available learning resources messaging to support the creation of development plans.

Also consider what is happening in your organization, industry, and broader economy when selecting the timing of your message. Communicating a message reflecting an expensive learning program at a time of decreasing sales could be detrimental to your learning function's alignment with the business. However, in a time when your business travel expenses are cut to accommodate decreasing sales, communicating a message highlighting your offerings of virtual learning classes shows much greater alignment.

The next column in the figure 5-1 matrix lists the effectiveness metrics for your communication efforts. Just as your business measures the effectiveness of its employee communications and marketing communications, you should similarly have effectiveness metrics for your communication. After all, you are spending time and money to communicate; it's logical that you would want to understand the effectiveness of your efforts. In addition, you can seriously undermine your alignment with the business by bombarding them with communication that adds little value and serves only as a distraction. In figure 5-1, one metric for communicating the launch of a new sales school is the amount of traffic driven to the new sales school website.

The figure 5-1 matrix concludes with the owner of the messaging implementation and target populations. Note how the prelaunch communication regarding the new sales school is sent to a broad audience of leaders. As the communication purpose evolves to reminding, the audience is highly targeted. The stakeholder analysis discussed in chapter 2 is helpful to segment your target audiences.

To execute your strategic communication plan, you must dedicate appropriate resources. Your budget should include funds for both the labor and communication media associated with implementing your plan. Though there is no precise rule of thumb, targeting 2 or 3 percent of your overall learning budget is a good start. For a reference point, industries such as retail and services allocate 2 or 3 percent of their gross sales for their marketing communication budgets. Highly competitive consumer products industries allocate greater amounts, such as 8 to 10 percent. The Expertus study (2008) cited above found that the average internal marketing budget for learning is only about 43 cents per employee per year. In comparison, a typical learning supplier may spend as much as $1,000 to get one person to purchase a seat in a class.

Your investment allocation should also factor in the maturity of your learning function. Newly launched or transforming learning functions will generally use greater amounts of strategic communication.

In the next section, we move from the overarching strategic communication plan to focus on specific, targeted content and formats for internal communication.

Using the Language of Business

Communication is happening all around us, with different objectives and an increasing variety of methods to communicate. The list of mobile communication devices continues to grow so long that rather than list them all, flight attendants now instruct passengers to "turn off *anything* with an on and off switch." This is a sign of the sheer volume of communication that surrounds us. Competition is intense to gain the attention and mindshare of those with whom we wish to communicate. Yet to truly drive the engagement and alignment of your learning function with business goals, you must gain your internal stakeholders' attention and mindshare.

The target of your communication is the receiver. Although this makes perfect sense, this focus can quickly disappear, if we communicate from a limited, learning-centric view. Overusing learning jargon can derail your communication.

To illustrate this point, see the sidebar for two comparative examples from the corporate university to leaders regarding the launch of a new sales school. Both examples were presented as possible drafts for senior learning manager approval before release.

Both examples given in the sidebar are valid forms of communicating the launch of a new leadership learning entity. However, as a business leader, which example would you prefer? Most business leaders would

Example A: " Learning Group Announces Sales Leadership Academy"

We are proud to announce the launch of our Sales Leadership Academy. This endeavor is the culmination of a year of research and planning. The focus of the academy is action learning. This is augmented with inductive design methods to accelerate competency development and relevancy of the content. Advanced instructional technology is used throughout the academy curriculum. Learning labs bring the learners together to focus on companywide issues. These documents are attached for your review:

- Academy Mission and Charter
- Adult Learning Principles for the Academy
- Action Learning Projects and Process
- Formative and Summative Evaluation Approaches.

Example B: "Sales Leadership Academy Launched to Increase Your Sales"

The Sales Leadership Academy—designed and created *by* our sales leaders *for* our sales leaders—is officially launched! Academy participants will work real business unit projects designed to increase sales while simultaneously learning how strengthen their sales leadership. The return for each business issue project must demonstrate a minimum of $100,000. To accommodate busy, global schedules, the academy uses mobile and virtual meeting tools to ensure that leaders have flexibility for when and where they learn. The two face-to-face learning sessions engage leaders from across the globe to collaboratively solve companywide business issues. A one-page frequently asked questions—FAQ—is provided for your reference.

prefer example B, because it focuses on why the Sales Leadership Academy is important to them. It also addresses what is important to them: solving real business issues with a minimal interruption of work flow. A cost performance metric of $100,000 or greater is included. By including this number, example B highlights that you recognize that the business focus is on increased sales. In other words, example B is focused on stakeholders, not focused on learning.

In example B, business rather than learning terms and phrases are used. Do most business leaders clearly understand "action learning," "inductive design methods," "competency development," or "instructional technology"? Probably not—nor do they really care about this professional jargon. The many attachments fall short in that they are focused on the learning function. In addition, how many busy business leaders have time to open and read four different, rather arcanely titled, documents? The simple FAQ attachment included with example B will help leaders communicate the launch and answer related questions.

You have probably surmised this, but example B was chosen as the final communication for release.

Segmenting Your Target Audiences for Communication

The comparative examples given in the sidebar were targeted to sales leaders. By virtue of their different roles and responsibilities, different levels of stakeholders have different communication requirements. It is important to segment (that is, to separate groups of people by shared characteristics) your target audiences and to customize your communication to their particular needs.

In her book *Quick! Show Me Your Value*, Theresa Seagraves (2004) provides examples of the financial content most pertinent to the four most common levels of business employee:

- senior leaders
- midlevel leaders
- first-level/operational leaders
- individual salespeople.

Using the example of a sales organization, let's look at the considerations involved in targeting each of these four segments in your communication plan.

Senior leaders, responsible for setting direction, are typically focused on multiyear strategy and the highest level of organizational metrics, such as profit margin (the difference in how much money comes in and how much money it costs to create, sell, and deliver the product or service). Senior leaders also attend more to the external world of stock shareholders, financial analysts, and financial markets. A possible title for this role is senior vice president, sales.

In this example, midlevel leaders are responsible for executing the direction and focus on achieving goals within a one- to three-year period. They typically coordinate a sales division and manage sales managers. A possible title for this role is vice president, sales. Continuing with the profit margin example, midlevel leaders are accountable for driving profitable sales and minimizing sales-driven costs that affect the company's profit. A midlevel leader will be concerned about sales activities that decrease profit, such as the overuse of pricing discounts. Given their role to execute strategy, a large part of the midlevel leader's role is communicating sales profitability performance to senior leaders.

First-level/operational leaders, such as sales managers, are responsible for managing the day-to-day work of selling. Their focus is typically a quarter up to a year timeframe. In our sales profit margin scenario, this role is focused on controlling the incorrect use of sales discounting. If salespeople overuse discounting rather than rely on their selling skills, profit margins drop. They will track the average discount rate per sales person.

Salespeople are the individual contributors who are engaged in selling to customers. They do not manage people and typically have an area of specialty sales knowledge or expertise. Salespeople are focused on meeting their sales quotas. To sell profitably, they will need to rely more on their selling skills than on price discounting to obtain the sale. Figure 5-2 summarizes the roles and business focus for these four levels of sales leadership.

Figure 5-2. The Roles and Business Focus for Four Levels of Sales Leadership

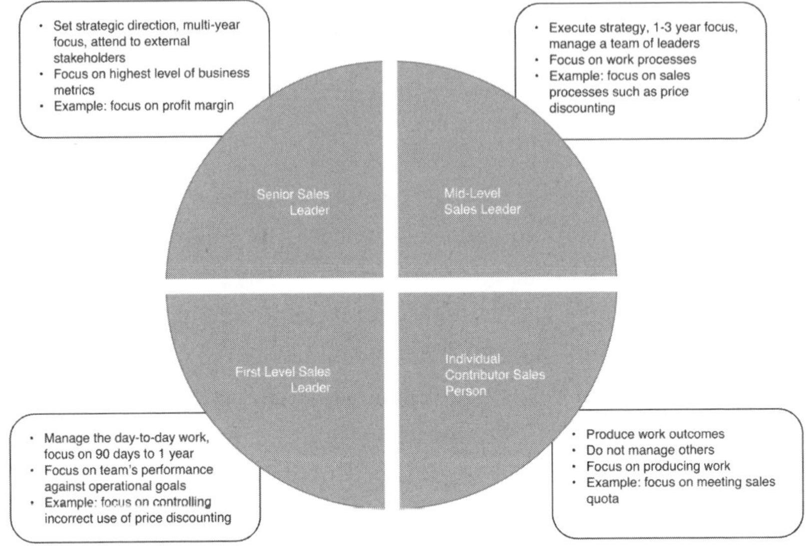

Case Example: Target Audience Segmentation

Let's look at how target audience segmentation can work in another similar context. The corporate university targets specific messaging and supporting data to the different levels of leaders in the company:

- Targeted for senior leaders, figure 5-3 is an excerpt from a metrics communication for a learning program tied directly to generating cash flow for the organization.
- Midlevel leaders in this company focus on the impact of the corporate university on their businesses. Figure 5-4 depicts an excerpt from an impact study targeted to midlevel sales and marketing leaders. Impact studies are distributed two to three times per year.
- First-level managers frequently focus on the participant costs charged to their business groups. In figure 5-5, curriculum costs are shown in a year-over-year comparison.

In a fashion similar to this segmenting, the stakeholder analysis work we considered in chapter 2 will help you segment and customize messages for your diverse stakeholders.

Crafting Your Messages

As students in academia, we were typically assigned to write research papers. We probably groaned when the teacher indicated that the paper was to be at least 20 pages in length. The communication we create in business environments is the exact opposite—concise writing is valued over length. The following adage rings true: A businessperson's attention span decreases the higher he or she ascends the corporate ladder.

Figure 5-3. Excerpt From a Metrics Communication for a Learning Program Tied to Generating Cash Flow

Cash Flow Metric Communication Targeted for Senior Leaders

In the Know on Cash Flow Metrics

Our goal was to create an effective online learning program that would reach all salaried employees with development completed and deployment started by end of Q3 to drive improvement in cash flow for 2009 and beyond.

Metric	**Measurement**	**Result**
Impact	Company Ability to Reach Cash Flow Targets	Currently forecasting available cash of $1.3B in 2009—20% above goal
Reach/Scope	Program Completions	17,100+ worldwide (12 languages)
Effectiveness	Participant Surveys	4.28 (on scale of 1.0 – 5.0) (Industry benchmark is 4.0)
Efficiency	Budget Adherence and Timeline	On budget and surpassed industry standards for rapid program development: (*Design and full deployment completed within six months.*)

Figure 5-4. Excerpt from an Impact Study Targeted to Midlevel Sales and Marketing Leaders

Table 1. Overall Impact of *IR Manager* Course

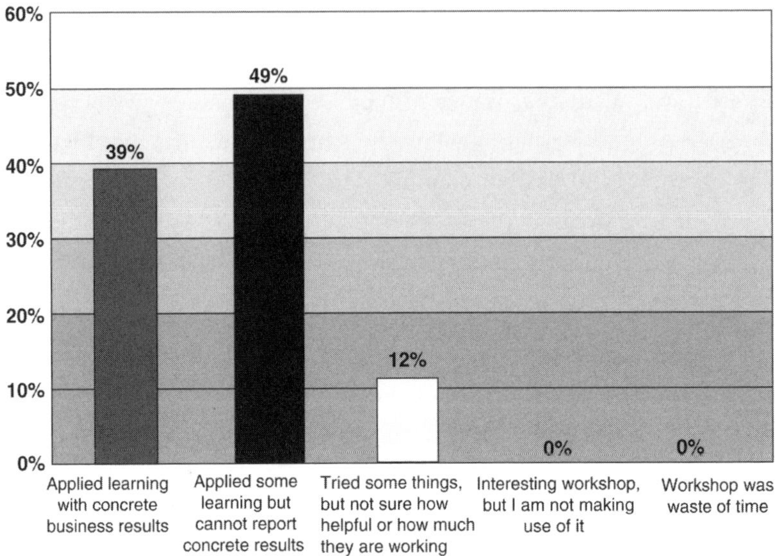

Successful business communication should be clear and concise. The communication should answer these questions for the recipient:

- What? (What is the message?)
- So what? (Why is this important to me?)
- Now what? (What action is required of me?)

Case Example: Business Format

In the magazine cover article depicted in figure 5-6, the corporate university is reinforcing its strategy of leaders as teachers (see chapter 4). Look for the "What? So what? Now what?" formula in this example:

- The *What?* is the message that leaders are engaged in corporate university learning solutions in a variety of roles, including leaders as teachers and visiting executives.

Figure 5-5. A Year-over-Year Comparison of Curriculum Costs for First-Level Managers

	Per Participant Cost - 2006	Per Participant Daily Rate - 2006	Per Participant Cost - 2007	Per Participant Daily Rate - 2007
Core Programs				
Business Acumen	$ 1,202.00	$ 400.67	$ 1,137.00	$ 379.00
Interpersonal Leadership Program	$ 2,745.00	$ 686.25	$ 902.00	$ 300.67
Process Excellence	$ 1,585.00	$ 317.00	N/A	N/A
Project Management Mastery	$ 1,215.00	$ 405.00	$ 1,092.00	$ 364.00
Roadmap for Change	$ 1,080.00	$ 360.00	$ 873.00	$ 291.00
Team Leadership	$ 1,113.00	$ 371.00	$ 785.00	$ 261.67
Strategic Change Workshop	$ 2,175.00	$ 435.00		
Leadership & General Management College				
Entrepreneurial General Manager Program	$ 5,526.00	$ 614.00	N/A	N/A
Aligning Your Organization for Global Advantage	$ 770.00	$ 385.00	$ 770.00	$ 385.00
Leader Level People Management	$ 2,381.00	$ 793.67	$ 2,042.00	$ 680.67
Adv. Leader Level People Management	$ 3,957.00	$ 989.25	$ 3,092.00	$ 773.00
Adv. Leader Level Business Management	$ 3,696.00	$ 924.00	$ 2,957.00	$ 739.25
Sales & Marketing College				
Advanced Pricing Workshop	$ 1,626.00	$ 542.00	$ 1,907.00	$ 635.67
Driving Dramatic Growth Through Marketing Excellence	$ 2,537.00	$ 507.40	$ 2,926.00	$ 585.20
Marketing for the IR Manager	$ 1,379.00	$ 459.67	$ 1,457.00	$ 485.67

[light shading] = Per person costs decreased from 2006 [dark shading] = Per person costs increased from 2006

*Decreases due to vendor optimization and increased utilization. Increases are in marketing programs that did not have cost reductions and had higher regional presence in 2007 than 2006.

- The *So what?* is how this leadership engagement keeps learning programs aligned and relevant to business needs and drives the desired culture of talent stewardship.
- The *Now what?* is to recognize the participating leaders as teachers who report to you.

Selecting Your Communication Method

When I first began in the learning profession, one of the few ways to communicate with stakeholders was face to face, by telephone, and by written newsletters and memos. There are many more communication methods today. Today, we use email, videoconferencing, instant messages, blogs, and social networking websites like Twitter to broadcast messages to the public and/or Yammer for private communication groups—to name just

Figure 5-6. External Communications: Feature Article

IMPROVING HUMAN PERFORMANCE

Grooming Leaders for Growth

Ingersoll Rand develops employees to have the time, energy, and business acumen to help grow the business.

By Rita Smith and Beth Bledsoe

IT MAY BE ONE of the most difficult questions that senior learning officers are grappling with today: How do we build a strong worldwide management team and our global business at the same time?

That question was also on the minds of leaders and corporate educators at Ingersoll Rand more than two years ago.

After selling heavy machinery equipment for more than 100 years, Ingersoll Rand transformed into a highly diversified company with $10.5 billion in annual revenues. During the past five years, the company has replaced, through acquisitions and divestitures, businesses comprising roughly $3 billion—one third of its annual revenues. Today, the company is in dozens of new markets, producing such products as biometric handreaders for airport security and refrigeration units for perishable food shipping.

Because of those changes, Ingersoll Rand has evolved financially, too. The company's revenues used to be in step with gross domestic product growth, but recently the company has experienced high single- and double-digit revenue increases, most of which are the result of acquiring shares in emerging markets, such as Asia and South America.

Acquiring leaders

Finding and retaining people with the appropriate skills, aptitude, and perspective to assume positions of leadership is a challenge for every organization. But for one una few. In the time it took to read this last sentence, a new communication technology was probably released. No matter what technology you choose to use, you always want to consider the following:

- your learning strategy
- the purpose of your communication message
- the characteristics of your targeted audience.

Case Example: Annual Report

Each year, the corporate university creates and distributes an electronic annual report to all the company's leaders. The format of your annual report should mirror that of your organization's annual report. It also reinforces accountability for performance results in exchange for investment in the corporate university. A company's annual report is published yearly and sent to company stockholders. The company appropriately views its stockholders as investors. The purpose of this company annual report is to provide investors with a summary of the year's performance and discuss direction for the upcoming year. The U.S. Securities and Exchange Commission, the federal agency responsible for enforcing stock industry laws and regulations, requires that all public companies issue an annual report. It is more than just a requirement; many companies also see their annual report as a marketing tool.

In this example, the corporate university similarly views its business leaders, who provide funding, as its "investors." Following the general format of most company-generated annual reports, the corporate university annual report includes:

- A letter from the chief learning office (or head of learning).
- Performance results for the corporate university in the company's strategic initiatives of productivity, innovation, generating cash flow, and engaging employees. To reinforce alignment with the business, the format of the annual report is categorized by these four strategic initiatives. Both qualitative and quantitative data is used. Photos of learning participants and graphics are used throughout

- A letter from the chief learning officer discussing the coming years' strategy for the corporate university.

The corporate university report is well received, and leaders share this communication with external stakeholders such as board members and employee candidates.

Case Example: Broad, Global Communications

To help drive the company's employee engagement strategy, the corporate university expanded its charter to include on-demand, online learning for all employees. Not every employee has direct access to a computer. Given variable computer access, a mix of communication methods was used to communicate this new learning solution. Methods included emails targeted to managers, electronic newsletter announcements, webinars, live meeting conference calls, posters, and brochures. Figure 5-7 depicts the English version of the posters hung in every company site around the globe. All materials were translated to ensure that non-English-speaking employees could fully participate.

Gathering Feedback From Your Customers

A strong communication system will build in opportunities for two-way communications. One key aspect of this is gathering regular feedback from the learning participants and their managers (our "customers"). Too often, learning professionals focus on programmatic feedback and gather only limited "voice of customer" feedback on the key learning processes. Of course, measuring the impact of learning requires you to capture and analyze feedback from participants and their management. There are many resources to guide you in measuring and communicating the impact of learning, including the works of Jack Phillips and Ron Stone (2002); Donald and James Kirkpatrick (2006); Robert Brinkerhoff (2003); and Cal Wick, Roy Pollack, and Andy Jefferson (2010).

However, measuring and communicating the efficiency and effectiveness of your learning processes is equally important and is the primary focus here. Processes include learning needs alignment, marketing and communication, production of learning solutions, relationship management, enrollment, delivery logistics, reporting, and the user's experience

Figure 5-7. The English Version of the Posters Hung in Every Company Site Around the Globe

Ingersoll Rand University
It's all about YOU!

with your learning technology. Your efficiency and effectiveness in performing these processes directly influences the business leader's overall satisfaction with your learning function. Process measures important to your business leaders could include

- speed: time to market for your learning solution
- reliability: operational learning technology
- usage: penetration/reach
- accuracy: the data integrity in your reporting
- costs: the comparative unit cost per learner
- usability: the process's ease for the learner
- alignment: the level of business relevance.

A good source of additional customer satisfaction metrics for your learning function appear in the Baldrige Award's Performance Excellence Criteria section. The Baldrige Award is an annual United States–based award designed to strengthen U.S. competitiveness in the world economy. Launched in 1987, it emphasizes a set of performance best practices and capabilities criterion from which a company can assess its own performance. The criteria are very specific and serve as an excellent guide for best practices.

Gathering feedback on your key processes is critical to drive continuous improvement and for regular assessments of your alignment with the business. Ideally, the voice of your customer should be integrated into your daily operations, rather than an annual event. To ensure your credibility and transparency and to obtain ongoing feedback, communicate feedback results and related improvements to the providers of the feedback.

There are multiple methods for gathering feedback on your processes. Web-based surveys are popular for the ease of use and reach. Integrate feedback tools such as Twitter directly into your processes to obtain real-time feedback. Another option is a Twitter link asking for immediate feedback, which could appear at the conclusion of the enrollment process. Host a feedback blog. Offer live chat support for certain key processes, and use this to gather feedback. Technology continues to provide us with an increasing range of feedback gathering communication. Using an independent third party is highly effective. Direct inquiry and focus groups, though more traditional, are equally as effective in gathering feedback.

Case Example: Feedback About the Online Learning Experience

The corporate university made a substantial investment in a library of online learning and is very interested in online learner feedback. An immediate web-based feedback survey is integrated into the completion of online learning programs. In addition to this data, a random survey of users who engaged in the online learning but who did not complete the program is deployed on a quarterly basis. Focus groups are also used. Figure 5-8 is a compilation of quarterly feedback analysis used to communicate online learning offerings to first-level and midlevel leaders.

Using an integrated approach to your communication strategy helps you keep focused on consistent, strategic messaging that drives your brand identity. Taking the time to create a strategic communication plan telegraphs the importance of strategic communication to the entire learning team. In addition, it fosters business-leader focus within the learning group. Finally, it provides measurable accountability for your strategic communication implementation.

External Communication

External communication is synonymous with public relations. The objective of external communication or public relations is to create a strong image of a company or, in this case, a learning function. Successful public relations can reach large audiences without the expense of traditional marketing efforts. The most common public relation vehicles include

- news releases
- press conferences
- sponsoring special events
- industry presentations
- awards
- interviews
- featured articles.

For a corporate university, external communication is important in building the reputation of your learning to external audiences. This, in turn, brings positive publicity to your company. Learning employees engaged in public relations experience recognition and pride as well. It is also a tool to recruit world-class learning professionals into your learning group. Featured articles and awards can be further leveraged for distribution to your internal audiences. External communication provides "benchmark sonar" for your business leaders on the comparative success and value of your corporate university amid the landscape of corporate universities.

Just as you did with internal communications, it is important to create an integrated, annual plan for external communication. Many people combine the internal and external plans into one macro plan. Regardless, a big-picture view will show potential gaps and opportunities and will help calendarize your public relations efforts.

Figure 5-8. Excerpt From a Compilation of Quarterly Feedback Analysis Used to Communicate Online Learning Offerings to First-Level and Midlevel Leaders

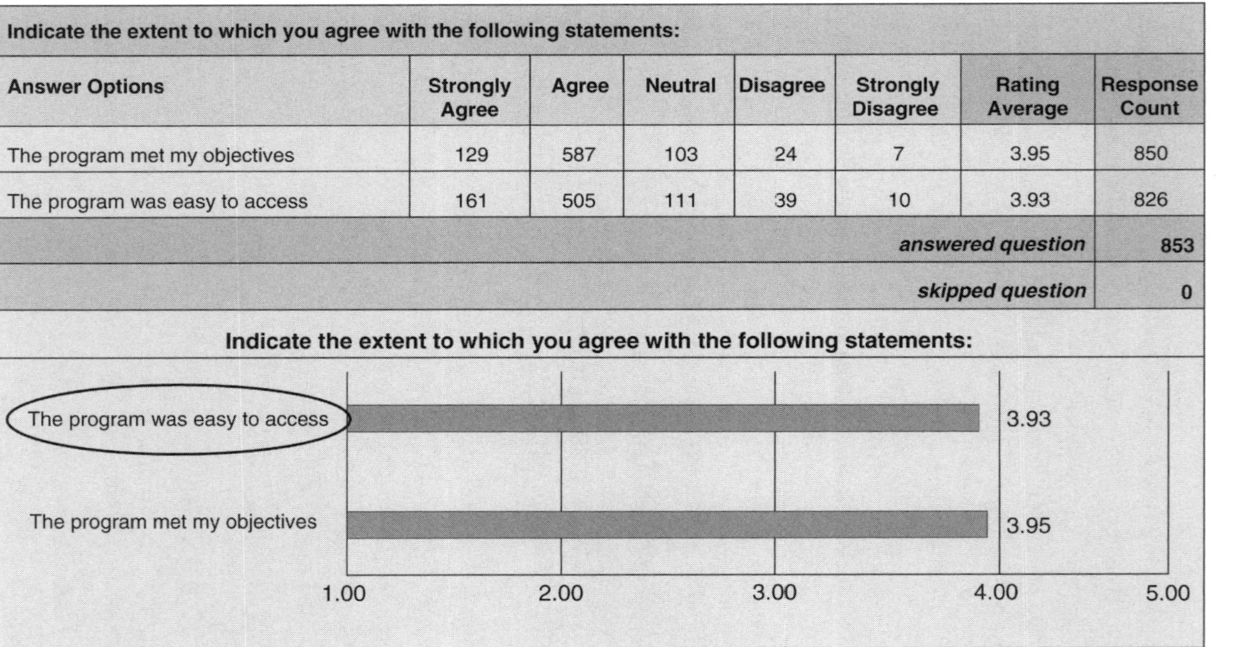

Voice of Customer Survey Data: Ease of Use for Online Learning

Use of Skillsoft Online Programs

Indicate the extent to which you agree with the following statements:							
Answer Options	**Strongly Agree**	**Agree**	**Neutral**	**Disagree**	**Strongly Disagree**	**Rating Average**	**Response Count**
The program met my objectives	129	587	103	24	7	3.95	850
The program was easy to access	161	505	111	39	10	3.93	826
						answered question	**853**
						skipped question	**0**

Now let's briefly consider a case example for an annual strategic external communication plan. The corporate university has been in operation for more than five years. It has a good internal reputation, but it wants to broaden this externally with increasing public relations. Its public relations strategy is excerpted in figure 5-9. The messaging and targeted activities are in alignment with and also drive the corporate university's strategy. For example, targeted external awards reinforce the corporate university's strategy to run the learning function as a business process. Figure 5-6 (see page 148) illustrates an external communicatons feature article.

Communicating with your business partners entails much more than publishing learning calendars—strategic communication can be used as a powerful tool for you to drive engagement and alignment with the business. The key is to create, execute, and measure an integrated

Figure 5-9. An Excerpt of the Corporate University's Public Relations Strategy

Annual Strategic Plan for External Communication

Corporate University—2011

AWARDS	ARTICLES
• ASTD Excellence in Practice • ASTD Best Award • Bersin Learning Leaders • Corporate University Exchange	• ASTD T+D Journal • Academy for Leadership Development • Engineering Journal • Wall Street Journal • CLO Magazine
INDUSTRY PRESENTATIONS	**SPONSOR SPECIAL EVENTS**
• ASTD International Conference & Expo Presentation—alignment • ASTD Charlotte Chapter—running learning as a business function • Electrical Engineering Annual Conference • CLO Best Practices Seminar	• Host ASTD benchmarking meeting • Financial sponsor for measurement research study

communication plan for your learning function. Your plan should be business-centric and guided by your learning strategy. Continually working this step of the Strategic Learning Alignment Model, *Communicating Your Business Results*, reinforces and advances your efforts in the model's three previous steps.

Key Points for Communicating Your Business Results

- Integrated planning and managing of your strategic communications is a powerful tool for you to create engagement and alignment with your business leaders.
- Use the language of business in your communications. Business communications should be clear, concise, and free of learning jargon.
- Segment your communication target audiences to ensure that you are providing them with communication that adds value to their specific role and business focus.
- To quickly gain the attention of your business leader, your communication should answer the following: What? So what? Now what?
- There are multiple methods to communicate. Regardless of the communication technology available, stick to the basics when selecting your method: Does it align with and advance with your learning strategy, is it congruent with your communication message, and does it align with the characteristics of your target audience?
- Your strategic communication should include the "voice of your stakeholders." Obtain and act on regular feedback, both on your learning products and solutions, and particularly on your learning processes.
- Create and manage an annual, macro plan for your external communications.

Exercises for Communicating Your Business Results

1. Using figure 5-1, an annual strategic communication plan template for internal communications, list one or two of your key strategic learning messages and work across the matrix. Did you need to create or refresh your communication metrics? How would you assess your learning function's performance against the communication metrics?

2. Use the *What? So what? Now what?* technique to create your next business leader communication. Compare this with previous communication samples. Do you see an observable difference in clarity and conciseness?

Chapter 6

A Call to Action for Learning Leaders

This book began with a self-assessment of your strategic alignment of the learning function with your business. This assessment typically creates a deeper awareness of the components of strategic learning alignment. The intent is that creating upfront awareness would guide your learning and action planning as you engaged with this book in the pages and exercises that followed.

Professionals involved in successful learning functions understand the components of alignment and combine them into a systematic process. In this book, the best practices for building business alignment with the learning function have been organized into an actionable system for learning leaders just like you.

The Strategic Learning Alignment (SLA) Model integrates the components of a four-step process of knowing your business, building the business case for learning, engaging stakeholders in key learning activities, and communicating your business results into a framework to help you create sustainable alignment with your business partners. This framework is based on the beliefs that learning is a business process and that learning professionals are both learning *and* business professionals.

Reflect for a moment on what the strategic alignment of the learning function with business goals could mean for your activities and position as a learning professional:

- A seat at the table for strategic business discussions and implications for learning—not an 11th-hour afterthought.

- Business leaders who articulate the value of learning in helping to achieve their business goals rather than constantly challenging their investment in learning.
- Business leaders who regard their engagement in the learning function's governing, designing, and teaching activities as a positive opportunity to ensure that learning is highly relevant to their business needs rather than a duty to avoid.
- Being regarded by your company as a mission-critical, business-credible function rather than as a cyclical expense.
- Participants who know that your learning solutions are relevant to the business and will involve valuable interaction with senior leaders, rather than participants viewing themselves as learning hostages.
- A transparent, business-leader-driven learning priority process that buffers you from constant bombardment with multiple training needs.
- Being externally recognized for your learning function as forming an integral part of your business rather than sitting on the learning sidelines.

These reflections are not fantasy or attainable by only a small handful of learning leaders. Any professionals involved in the learning function can make this a reality.

You may work in a company where the top leaders view learning as a "nice to have" and a ready target for budget cuts. However, even in this environment, you can make progress by beginning with step 1 of the SLA Model, *Knowing Your Business*. When you truly understand how your business makes money and tracks performance, you have cracked opened the door to the executive boardroom. You are able to articulate how learning can help your business leaders achieve their goals. You are, therefore, more likely to catch their attention and interest. Using your stakeholder analysis information, you can target specific business leaders and work to address their corresponding business issues. Start with those stakeholders who will be more receptive to your efforts. There is a multiplicative effect in gaining the support of even a handful of business leaders. What business leader would not want the learning function to generate a positive return on their investment by being aligned with their business needs?

You may have cracked open the boardroom door, but how do you move from a handful of generally receptive business leaders to earn the respect of your company's financial leaders? Step 2 of the SLA Model, *Building the Business Case for Learning*, helps you present your function as the provider of a value-added business process. By using this SLA step, you can co-create a strategic learning plan and funding requests with your business leaders and present them in the language and analytics used by your financial leaders. Financial leaders will thus begin to view your learning function in a different light. And when these financial leaders understand learning's business value and trust your financial management of learning, you will have succeeded in stepping through the boardroom threshold.

This is definitely progress. But how do you move to a true seat at the boardroom table? You can accomplish this with step 3 of the SLA Model, *Engaging Leaders in Key Learning Activities*. By engaging your business leaders in the governance of the learning function, in the development of learning solutions, and in serving as teachers, you will create learning that is aligned with business priorities. You are inviting your business leaders into your learning function to share the ownership and impact of the learning solutions. This approach allows you to engage a broad base of leaders who will likely become advocates for the value and business relevance of your learning function. Entering an executive boardroom with a financial leader's support and a business leader as your advocate earns you an invitation to sit at and participate at the boardroom table.

To sustain your seat at the boardroom table, you will need to consistently maintain your business leaders' mindshare in the value of learning. By following step 4 of the SLA Model, *Communicating Your Business Results*, you can achieve this. Building on your knowledge of the business, operating with the financial language and tools of business, and creating business-owned learning functions set the stage to communicate your business results. Using an integrated communication plan helps you target specific stakeholders with business-relevant messaging. In addition, by ensuring that you have two-way communication, you can gather feedback from the critical voices of your business customers. This feedback will enable you to continually improve the learning solutions, processes, and impact you provide to your business.

As you can see, creating strategic learning alignment is a process and not an event. As with any business process, creating and sustaining strategic alignment requires ongoing planning, execution, management, and time. With the proverbial seat at the boardroom table as your target, your efforts can deliver highly valuable outcomes. Given the ongoing nature of strategic learning alignment, every learning leader who reads this book still has work to do.

Using the SLA Model self-assessment and framework, what work will you do to create unparalleled alignment with your business leaders? As you put this book down, what is your most important, immediate first step to create unprecedented alignment of learning with your business partners?

Key Steps—One Person's Perspective

Your first step could be to increase your understanding of how your business makes money. This was my first step. At the time, I was a learning professional in the airline industry. It is important to note here that I was a liberal arts major whose previous knowledge of the airlines was winter trips to Florida. I obviously had a lot to learn. First, I completed some background research on the airline industry to understand key concepts, like "load factor" (the percentage of available seats filled) and "aircraft utilization" (the average number of hours an aircraft flies in a 24-hour period). Despite the fact that the flight attendants often voiced pleasure at a light number of customers to serve, I learned that it was important for the airline to have full planes with every available seat filled. An empty seat is considered waste and generates no revenue. I also learned that anytime an aircraft is on the ground, this expensive equipment is not making money for the company. I sought out seasoned pilots and the corporate finance managers to better understand the airline industry. I was far from an expert, but I was gaining a business view of why the learning function existed at this airline company.

I will never forget one of my first executive-level presentations to the airline business leaders when I was presenting a request for training funds. I delivered my request in the language of the airline business. I was able to link the recommended learning solutions to decreasing open seats on flights and how to decrease the "turn time" (the time it takes to deplane passengers, service the plan, and enplane new passengers) for aircraft parked at the terminal gates. When I completed my presentation, there was a pause, and then heads nodded in approval. Although this occurred many years ago, I will never forget their slightly surprised reaction. They were pleasantly surprised that I could speak their language—the language of business. And so my journey began.

Over the years, I obtained an MBA, something I never would have considered before starting my quest to understand the business world around me. Through years of networking, I found other learning professionals who also sought alignment with their business leaders through understanding and using the language of business. I spent many years trying to identify and replicate the best practices I witnessed from these other business-centered learning functions. The Strategic Learning Alignment Model introduced in this book captures these best practices in one place and provides you with a systematic way to create a powerful strategic partnership with your business leaders. By investing your time in reading this book, you've already accelerated your understanding of business. In the language of business, put this knowledge to work today to ensure that you get a good return on your investment.

Tips From Chief Learning Officers

Finally, here are inspiring first-person tips from successful chief learning officers:

> A clear understanding of the value proposition learning brings to our company is critical for our sustained success. At Yum! University, our value proposition is focused on building people capability across our system in three clearly defined areas: cultural excellence, leadership excellence, and functional excellence. We know that real value is defined not by

our perception but instead through the eyes of our partners, regardless of where they may be in our system. As a result, we continually seek feedback from our partners on how effectively we are adding value. We stop doing things when it is clear that our customers don't value it—regardless of how great an "idea" we might think it is. Each Yum! University learning professional is focused on ensuring that what they do brings our value proposition to life. Our goal is that the partners we serve can clearly see the value we provide their business.

—Rob Lauber, chief learning officer, YUM! Brands

I'm fortunate. I am welcomed into 20 or 30 organizations each year. When I visit, almost always it is at the invitation of the learning organization and its leadership. Often, we speak of how important it is for learning people to be riveted by the nature of their business, whatever that business is. I don't think I've ever heard a single disagreement with the tenet that learning people need to know what business they are in, at a level that goes beyond bumper stickers, and that they must act on that knowledge in ways that are frequent and meaningful.

If there is no disagreement, why isn't it typical? I think it goes to clarity of expectations first and metrics second.

First, expectations. Has learning leadership said that it is expected? Have they said what it would look like? Do they themselves manifest knowledge of the business, strategy, competitors? When decisions are made, do they link those decisions to the nature of the business and to metrics that particularly matter to a financial services company versus a manufacturer versus the professional development arm within a community college system? The learning organization develops its people on topics related to learning and performance. Do they do the same for the business of their business? What do they expect to be different as a result of journal subscriptions, podcasts, or conference attendance?

Then there is metrics. What are the metrics that will matter most to the business? Have they been discussed? Are they designed into systems? Are they captured? Are they used? Does learning leadership point to efforts that have been particularly meaningful in their organization, say, retention in the community colleges or repeat business in financial services? Metrics must matter, and that matteringness hails from one source: congruence with the essence of the business.

—Allison Rossett, professor emerita,
San Diego State University

Communicating my learning group's impact on the business is an ongoing process. We regularly create learning impact studies to share with our hospital's leadership. A best practice for us in communicating our impact is to start with our *executives' definition of success and set targets*—priorities for development are based on the strategic plan and the annual operating plan. Then we specifically determine outcomes expected for learners and customers (patients and families). We confirm the *directed investment in education* with the Education Steering Committee. We also determine generic and customized reports by discussing the *audience and purpose for those reports*, such as certification, compliance, performance, strategic plan progress, training catalog content management, application of learning on the job, cost benefit, and return on investment. Several *mechanisms are used to communicate results and outcomes* enterprisewide: monthly dashboard, quarterly progress report, and at regular presentations to the (internal) Education Steering Committee and the (community and executive) Education Committee of the Board of Trustees. There will always be opportunities to reuse your data. Reports and presentations include the link to training purpose (remember those definitions of success and targets), progress over time (use run charts), and recommendations for next steps, new targets, or new goals. We have *aligned expectations and shared appreciation of cumulative (long-term) effects* of learning and development.

—Rebecca Phillips, vice president, education and learning, and associate professor, Division of General and Community Pediatrics, Cincinnati Children's Hospital Medical Center

Education and training are key to our continued success at Oracle. With more than 60 acquisitions in the last five years, it is critical to onboard all the new employees rapidly. A key component is "field readiness," where we train, track, and certify our sales, consulting, and field engineering teams to be prepared for new product releases. Working closely with each business unit, we craft development and training plans customized to each geography in the world. A strong learning governance structure lets us maximize our lean infrastructure for maximum return.

—John L. Hall, senior vice president, Oracle University

There is a strong case for engaging business leaders in the strategic governance of your corporate university. Research conducted via CorpU with our member companies continues to point to governance as a major lever in creating strategic alignment of learning with the business. A best practice in learning governance is to create a structure that maximizes efficiencies across common critical programs, methods, processes, and technologies and leaves to business units those programs that are specific to their requirements.

—Ed Skonecki, vice president,
Corporate University Xchange

As the chief human resources officer of Darden, I have the learning function in my portfolio. Understanding business is core to creating and delivering valued learning and development solutions to enable our business success. Learning professionals need to understand the business strategy, how the business makes money, key business metrics, industry dynamics, workforce dynamics, and how people play in the equation of business success. One of the best examples of learning professionals applying understanding of business is the development of our "Manager in Training Program"—where the team needs to design a program that can replicate the real restaurant environment and scenario. In addition, the team is capable to articulate and quantify the impact to our bottom line—including the acceleration of leadership readiness—time to market.

—Daisy Ng, senior vice president and chief human resources officer, Darden Restaurants, Inc.

For decades, we have been saying training must be run like a business. How can you run a successful business without knowing your client's problems, language, culture, and top priorities? In this new normal environment, businesses must add value to their clients to achieve client satisfaction and retention. This is also true for training and learning. You need to be at the table when the business uses its strategy tools and processes to determine the company's product, services, goals, and performance issues. If you are not at their table, you could wind up on their menu.

—Sandy Quesada

References and Further Reading

Aberdeen Group, Inc. 2006. The Product Profitability "X Factor." *The Product Lifecycle Collaboration Benchmark Report*, June 3–4. www.oracle.com/partners/en/058849.pdf.

Berman, Karen, and Joe Knight, with John Case. 2008. *Financial Intelligence for HR Professionals: What You Really Need to Know About the Numbers*. Boston: Harvard Business Press.

Bersin, Josh. 2010. *Informal Learning: What, Why, and How—The Economic Realities.* www.bersin.com/Lib/Rs/Details.aspx?docid=103312462&title=Informal-Learning-What-Why-and-How—The-Economic-Realities&id=.

Betof, Edward. 2009. *Leaders as Teachers: Unlock the Teaching Potential of Your Company's Best and Brightest.* Arlington, VA, and San Francisco: ASTD Press and Berrett-Koehler.

Bingham, Tony, and Pat Galagan. 2007. *A View from the Top: How CEOs Link Learning to Corporate Strategy*. Arlington, VA: ASTD Press.

Brinkerhoff, Robert O. 2003. *The Success Case Method: Find Out Quickly What's Working and What's Not*. San Francisco: Berrett-Koehler.

Brinkerhoff, Robert O., and Anne M. Apking. 2001. *High Impact Learning: Strategies for Leveraging Business Results from Training*. Cambridge, MA: Perseus.

Business Literacy Institute. 2010. *Maps for Learning*. www.business-literacy.com/moneymaps-new.html.

Cooper, Robert G. 1986. *Winning at New Products Accelerating: The Process from Idea to Launch*. New York: Addison-Wesley.

Dressner, Marcia. 2010. Learning Governance and Structure: Results from the 10th Annual Benchmarking Study. http://corpu.com/documents/ResearchBrief_Governance.pdf.

Expertus, Inc. 2008. *Survey Results Training Efficiency: Internal Marketing, 2008*. Training Efficiency Masters Series. www.trainingefficiency.com/system/files/Survey+Results_Marketing+Training+Internally_Expertus.pdf.

Gardner, Howard. 1996. *Leading Minds: An Anatomy of Leadership*. New York: Basic Books.

Hall, Brandon. 2005. The Top Training Priorities for 2005. *Training*, February, 2.

Kirkpatrick, Donald L., and James D. Kirkpatrick. 2006. *Evaluation Training Programs: The Four Levels*, 3rd ed. San Francisco: Berrett-Koehler.

Mankowski, Diana, and Jose Raissa. 2003. *The 70th Anniversary of FDR's Fireside Chats*. Museum of Broadcast Communications. www.museum.tv/exhibitionssection.php?page=79.

O'Donovan, Gabrielle. 2003. A Board Culture of Corporate Governance. *Corporate Governance International Journal* 6, no. 3: 28–37.

Osterwalder, Alexander, and Yves Pigneur. 2009. *Business Model Generation: A Handbook for Visionaries, Game Changers, and Challengers*. New York: John Wiley & Sons. Available at www.businessmodelgeneration.com.

Phillips, Jack, and Ron Stone. 2002. *How to Measure Training Results*, 2nd ed. New York: McGraw-Hill.

Ramelli, Daniel. 2008. Learning Linked to Business Results. In *ASTD Handbook for Workplace Learning Professionals*, edited by Elaine Biech. Arlington, VA: ASTD Press.

Seagraves, Theresa. 2004. *Quick! Show Me Your Value: A Trainer's Guide to Communicating Value, Connecting Training and Performance to the Bottom Line*. Arlington, VA: ASTD Press.

Tichy, Noel M., and Nancy Cardwell. 2004. *The Cycle of Leadership: How Great Leaders Teach Their Companies to Win*. New York: HarperCollins.

Todd, Sue. 2009. *CorpU: Designing the Optimal Organization Structure & Governance Model*. www.corpu.com/research/designing-optimal-organization-structure-and-governance-model/.

van Reil, Cees B. M., and Charles J. Fombrun. 2007. *Essentials of Corporate Communication Implementing Practices for Effective Reputation Management.* New York: Routledge.

Walton, Jim. 2010. *Developing a Marketing Communications Budget: Are You Adequately Funding Your Promotional Machine?* Inside Indiana Business. Com. www.insideindianabusiness.com/contributors.asp?id=1179.

Wick, Calhoun W., Roy V. H. Pollack, and Andy Jefferson. 2010. *The Six Disciplines of Breakthrough Learning.* San Francisco: Pfeiffer.

About the Author

Rita Mehegan Smith, EdD, MBA, is vice president of enterprise learning for Ingersoll Rand—a $14 billion global, diversified industrial company—and dean of Ingersoll Rand University, which is responsible for developing strategic organizational competencies, providing leadership education, and driving the company's culture around the globe. She has served for more than 28 years in leadership roles in the learning and development field and has led learning functions in a variety of Fortune 500 companies in industries such as travel, financial services, and high technology manufacturing. She is currently on the Advisory Board for the Wharton School's chief learning officer program. She is a certified Toastmaster and frequently shares her knowledge and passion for business-centered learning at global workshops and conferences. In November 2008, Ingersoll Rand University and Ingersoll Rand's CEO were featured on the cover of *T+D* magazine, highlighting the university's business alignment and impact.

Index